Contents

How to Use *Daily Summer Activities*

Provide Time

Every day make sure that your child has a quiet time for practice. The practice session should be short and successful. Consider your child's personality and other activities as you decide how to schedule daily practice periods.

Provide Materials

Your child will need a quiet place to work. Put extra writing and drawing paper, scissors, crayons, pencils, and a glue stick in a tub or box. Store the supplies and *Daily Summer Activities* in the work area you and your child choose.

Provide Encouragement and Support

Your response is important to your child's feelings of success. Keep your remarks positive. Recognize the effort your child has made. Correct mistakes together. Work toward independence, guiding practice when necessary.

Track Progress

Each weekly section begins with a record form. Have your child color the symbols as each day's work is completed.

What's in *Daily Summer Activities*?

Ten Weekly Sections

Each of the ten weekly sections provides basic skill practice in several subject areas. The practice sessions are short, giving your child a review of what was learned during the previous school year.

Weekly Record Form

In addition to providing a means to record work completed, the record form also contains:

- a reading log where your child records the number of minutes read each day (See pages 4 and 5 for reading suggestions.)
- a weekly spelling list
- a place where your child can record interesting daily events

Reading
Your child will review consonant and short vowel sounds, and read words, phrases, and sentences. He or she will also read short stories and answer questions to show comprehension. Have your child read each story aloud to an adult or a sibling for additional practice. Encourage your child to attempt to figure out words that are unfamiliar, but do offer help if your child appears frustrated. For example, you might ask, "What word that begins with *p* might make sense in this sentence?" or "You know that this part of the word says *and*. Can you add the rest of the word?"

Language Skills
Your child will practice phonetic and other word attack skills as well as develop new vocabulary.

Math
Your child will practice counting, computation, and other appropriate math concepts each week.

Spelling
Each weekly record form includes two spelling words to learn. Have your child practice the spelling words in several ways: copy them several times, write them from memory, and spell them aloud. On Friday, ask your child to spell the week's words. This testing may be done orally or in writing. Add any missed words to the next week's spelling list for additional practice. A compiled spelling list can be found on page 143.

Handwriting
Your child will write letters, words, and sentences, using good handwriting. A chart showing correct letter formation is included on page 7.

Geography Readiness
This weekly activity involves using positional words, reading grids, and identifying a map. Each of these exercises will help ready your child for more complex geography skills.

Drawing and Writing
Each week your child will draw something and then write about it. This creative experience is an opportunity for your child to begin expressing ideas in written form. This is not a time to worry about spelling or correct sentence structure.

Encourage Reading

Be a Model

The most important thing you can do for your child is to read.

Read to your child—Visit libraries and bookstores, and read your way through museums, parks, stores, and playgrounds.

Read by yourself—It is important that your child see you reading. Read books, magazines, and newspapers. Read signs, labels, letters, directions, and displays as well.

Two Kinds of Reading

Shared Reading

Sit with your child. Take turns reading. You read a page; your child reads a page. Read with feeling.

Stop reading occasionally and ask your child to predict what will happen next. Listen carefully and then read on to see if the prediction was correct.

Independent Reading

Independent reading for children just beginning to read involves looking through familiar and new books, using the details in pictures to help with comprehension, retelling the story, and beginning to read words and sentences.

Talking About Reading

Check your child's understanding of what is read in a number of ways:

1. When you and your child have finished reading a story, ask your child to tell what the story was about.
2. Have your child draw a picture or write a word on an index card to represent the important things that happened in the story. Put the cards in order to show the sequence of events.
3. Ask your child to make up a new adventure for the characters in the story or to invent a different ending. Write the adventure and add pictures.

Helping Your Child Select Appropriate Books

An appropriate book for a beginning reader should have appealing pictures that give clues to the story. These picture clues will expand the plot and help your child figure out new words. The topic should be of interest to your child. The book should have clear, easy-to-read text. The story should encourage retelling.

Books to Read

ABC Pop! by Rachel Isadora; Viking Children's Books, 1999.

Are You My Mother? by P. D. Eastman; Random House, 1988.

At the Pond (Look Once, Look Again) by David M. Schwartz; Gareth Stevens, 1999.

Barnyard Banter by Denise Fleming; Henry Holt & Company, Inc., 1994.

Brown Bear, Brown Bear, What Do You See? by Eric Carle; Henry Holt & Company, Inc., 1996.

Buzz Said the Bee (Hello Reader, Level 1) by Wendy Cheyette Lewison; Scholastic Trade, 1992.

Chicka Chicka Boom Boom by John Archambault & Bill Martin, Jr.; Simon & Schuster, 1991.

Cloudy Day, Sunny Day (Green Light Readers) by Donald Crews; Green Light Readers, 1999.

Cookie's Week by Cindy Ward; Demco Media, 1992.

Count by Denise Fleming; Henry Holt & Company, Inc., 1997.

Don't Forget the Bacon by Pat Hutchins; Greenwillow, 1987.

Each Orange Had 8 Slices: A Counting Book by Paul Giganti; Mulberry Books, 1999.

Fox Box by Edward Marshall; Puffin, 1996.

Goldilocks and the Three Bears (Ready-to-Read) by Betty Miles; Simon & Schuster, 1998.

Green Eggs and Ham by Dr. Seuss; Random House, 1960.

Hop on Pop by Dr. Seuss; Random House, 1963.

If You Give a Mouse a Cookie by Laura Joffe Numeroff; HarperCollins Juvenile Books, 1985.

I Read Signs by Tana Hoban; William Morrow & Co. Paper, 1987.

Lunch by Denise Fleming; Henry Holt, 1998.

One Fish Two Fish Red Fish Blue Fish by Dr. Seuss; Random House, 1981.

Parade by Donald Crews; Greenwillow, 1983.

The Three Billy Goats Gruff by Stephen Carpenter; HarperCollins Juvenile Books, 1998.

Tuesday by David Wiesner; Clarion Books, 1997.

26 Letters and 99 Cents by Tana Hoban; Mulberry Books, 1995.

Where's Spot? by Eric Hill; Putnam Publishing Group Juvenile, 1990.

Who Hops? by Katie Davis; Harcourt, Inc., 1998.

Learning Excursions

Take an Excursion

Learning takes place everywhere. Take advantage of all the opportunities around you to increase your child's learning. At home, in the car, while shopping, or on special outings, talk about what you see, ask questions, and look for answers. These experiences help your child develop a richer vocabulary, learn new concepts, and have a better understanding of the world.

Here are ten learning excursions you and your child might experience together. These suggestions are only the beginning. Add others that occur to you.

1. Go to the public library every week to check out books.
2. Take nature walks. Look, listen, and touch to explore the outdoors. Take along a magnifying glass to look at small insects and plant parts. Keep a log of the animals and plants you see.
3. Go out on a clear night and look at the stars. Find the Big Dipper.
4. Go shopping together. Compare prices of items to be purchased.
5. Explore various types of stores. Help your child name various items. For example, visit a hardware store. Name the different types of tools and talk about how they are used. Then provide opportunities for your child to use some of the tools.
6. Explore your community. Identify the different types of buildings and landmarks.
7. Visit an older relative. Talk about the old days. How are things different now?
8. Start a collection.
9. Build, sew, or cook something new. This should include determining what is needed to complete the project and going to the store to purchase the materials.
10. Tour local businesses to learn more about your community.

After the Excursions

There are many interesting and fun ways for your child to extend what is learned on the excursions.

1. Write about the excursion in the "What Happened Today?" section of the weekly record form.
2. Make lists or draw pictures of interesting places visited, animals seen, or new experiences.
3. Make a scrapbook of photos, items collected from nature, keepsakes, etc. Label the items to identify them and to tell where they were obtained. This is a wonderful way to remember summer events.
4. Write letters to friends and family members to tell about these summer adventures.
5. Write and illustrate a story about the excursion.
6. Mark excursions on a calendar to keep track of where you've been and what you've done.

Note: Tear this out and post it to help you make your letters correctly.

Manuscript Writing

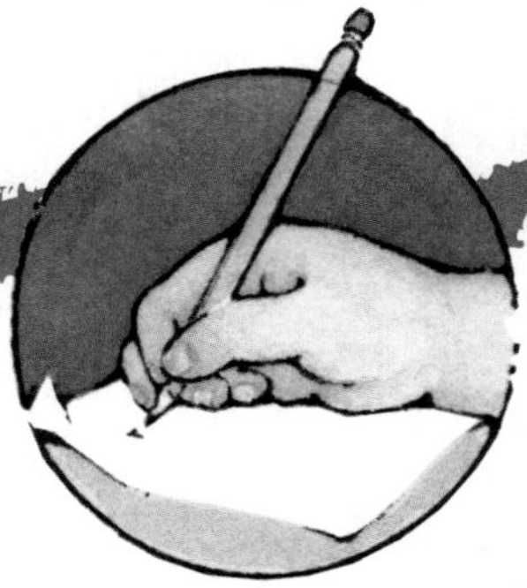

Aa Bb Cc Dd

Ee Ff Gg Hh

Ii Jj Kk Ll

Mm Nn Oo Pp

Qq Rr Ss Tt

Uu Vv Ww Xx

Yy Zz

WEEK 1

Color a ☆ for each page finished.

			Parent's Initials
Monday	☆	☆	________
Tuesday	☆	☆	________
Wednesday	☆	☆	________
Thursday	☆	☆	________
Friday	☆	☆	________

Spelling Words

stop

go

What Happened Today? Write about one thing you did each day.

Monday ________________________________

____

____

Tuesday ________________________________

____

____

Wednesday ________________________________

____

____

Thursday ________________________________

____

____

Friday ________________________________

____

____

Keeping Track Color a book for every 10 minutes you read.

Monday	Tuesday	Wednesday	Thursday	Friday

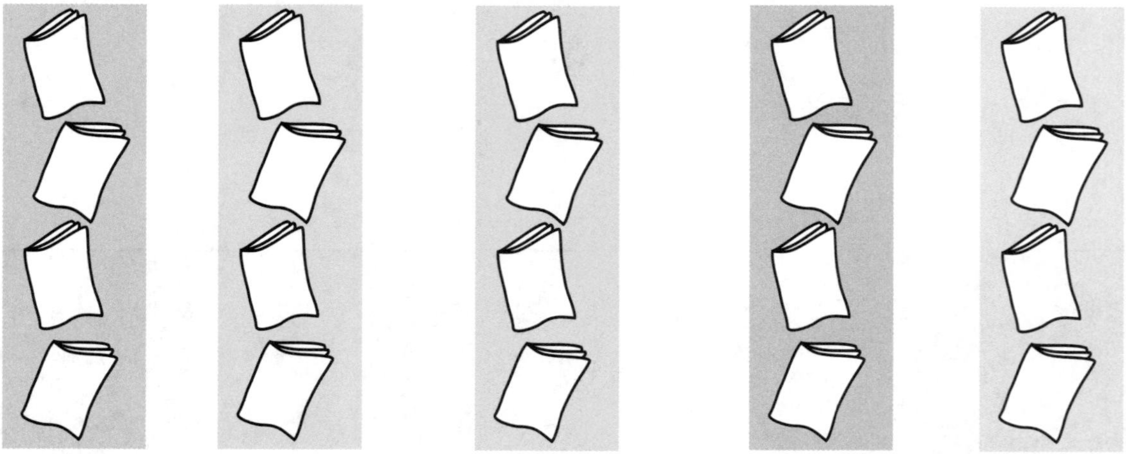

Bb

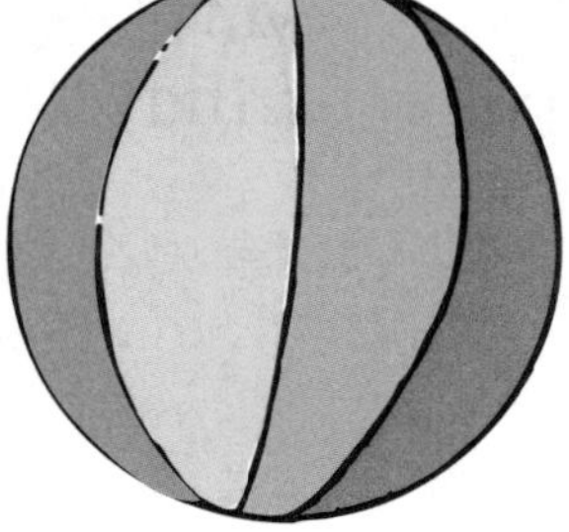

Trace and Write

b b b B B B

Which pictures begin with the sound made by the letter b?
Color them red.

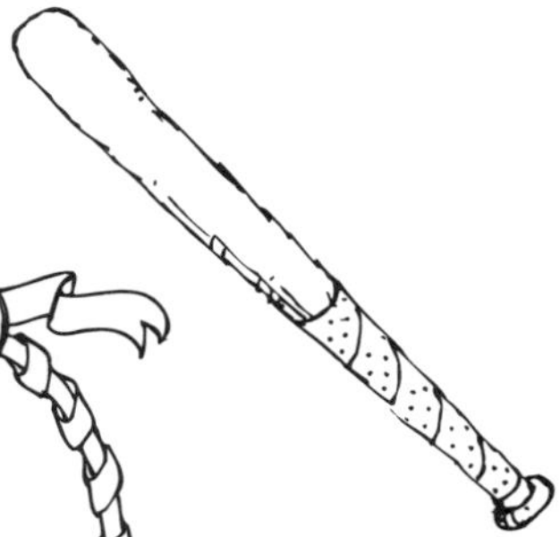

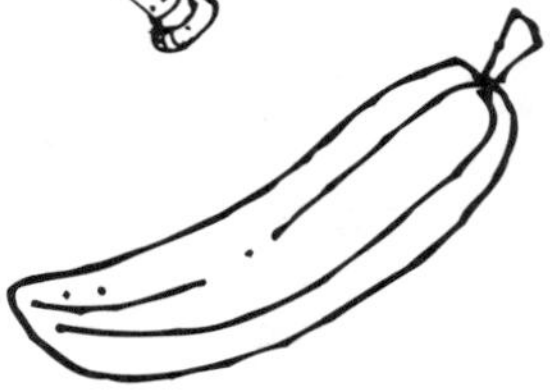

Make an X on the pictures that **begin** with the same sound.

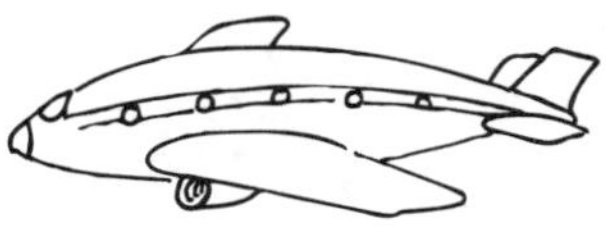
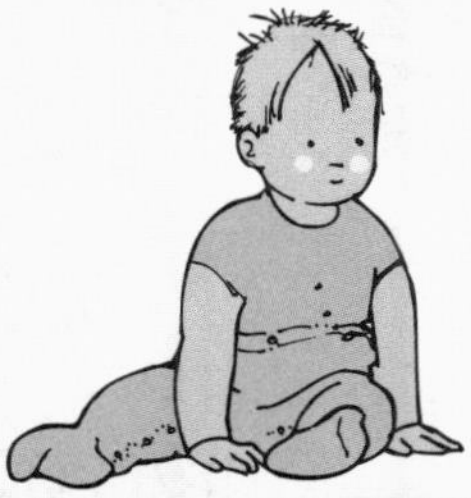
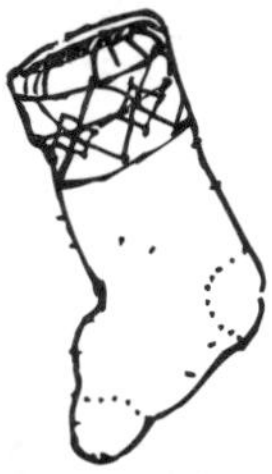

Color the pictures that rhyme.
Make an **X** on the pictures that do **not** rhyme.

Trace and Write

1 1 1 1

2 2 2 2

3 3 3 3

4 4 4 4

5 5 5 5

Count to 10 for an adult. **I can count to 10.** yes no

Spell It!

Practice spelling **stop** and **go**.

Write a letter in each box.

go stop

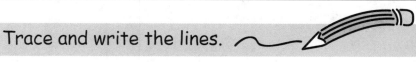

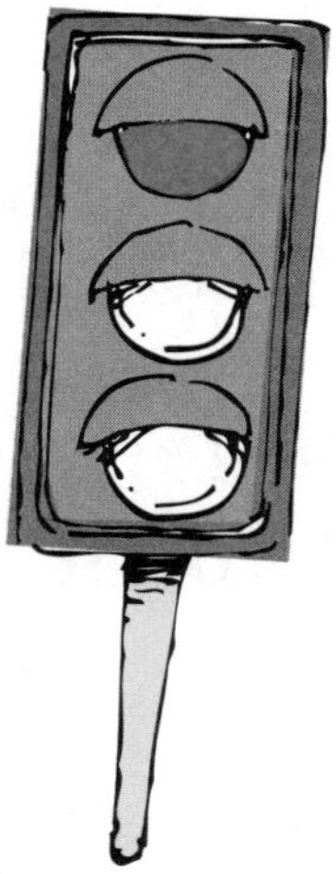

go

Trace and write the words.

stop

go

Trace and write the lines.

Tuesday

Week 1

Make an **X** on the one that is **different** in each row.

One fish in each bowl.

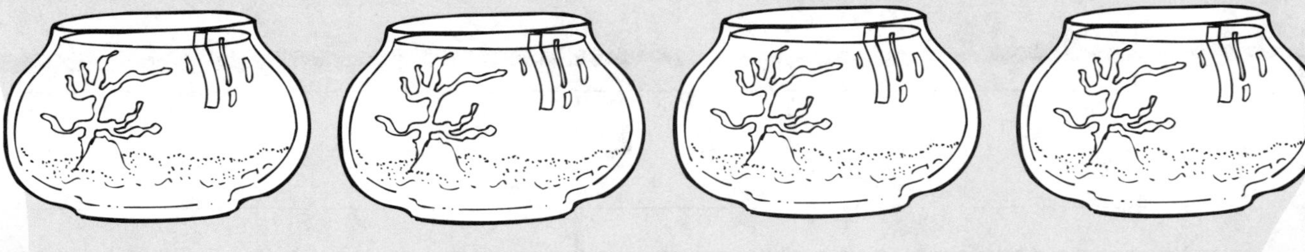

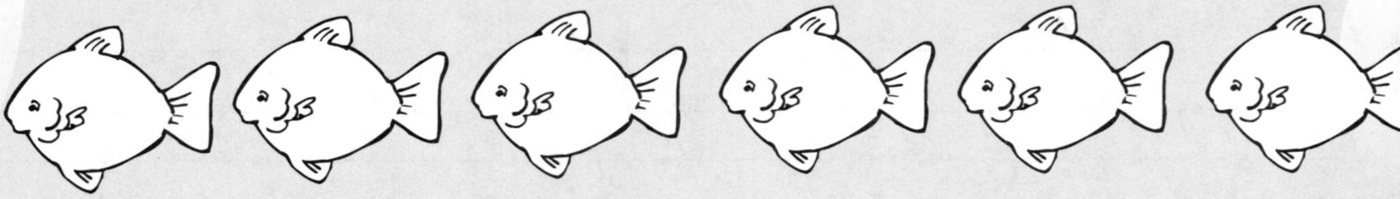

Are there enough bowls? yes no

In the Fruit Bowl

1 green pear,

2 red apples,

3 yellow bananas,

and purple grapes.

Yum!

Match and color.

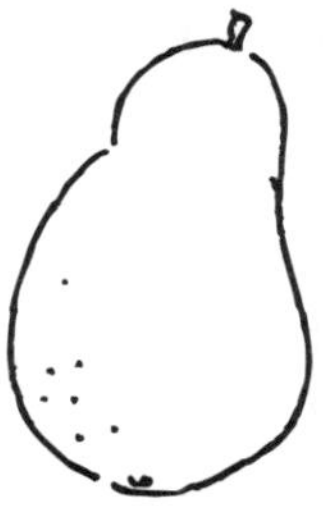

red

yellow

green

black

orange

purple

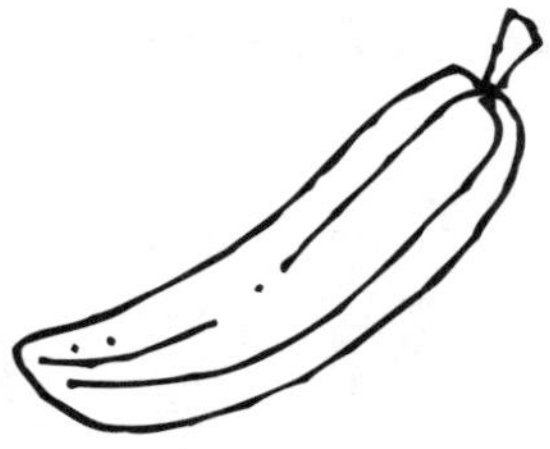

Cc

Trace and Write

c c c

C C C

Which pictures begin with the sound made by the letter c?
Color them blue.

1 ● 2 ▲ 3 ■ Color to finish the patterns.

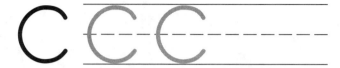

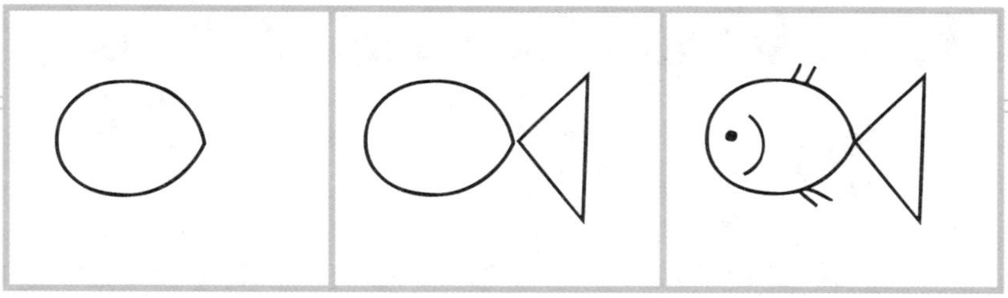

Draw a fish.

A fish can ______________________________ .

WHERE IS IT?

Circle the answers.

	in on		in on
	in on		in on
	in on		in on

What Goes Together?

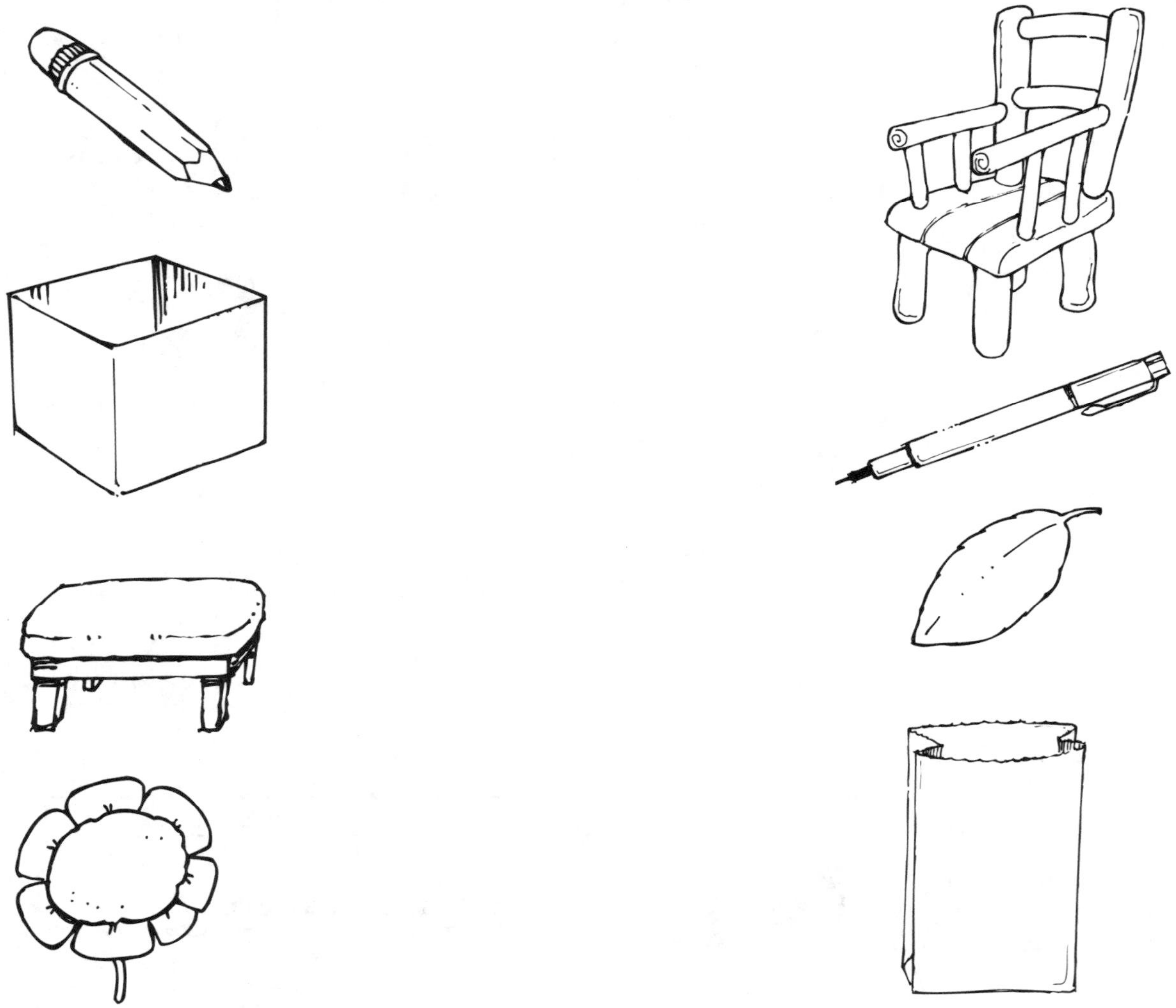

MATH TIME

Count the money.

________¢ ________¢ ________¢

A B C Touch each letter and read it to an adult. X Y Z

a b c d e f g h i j k l m

n o p q r s t u v w x y z

I can name [ ] letters.

● 1 ● +1	●● 2 ● +1	●●● 3 +0
●● 2 ●● +2	0 ●● +2	● 1 ●●● +3
● 1 +0	●●● 3 ● +1	● 1 ●● +2

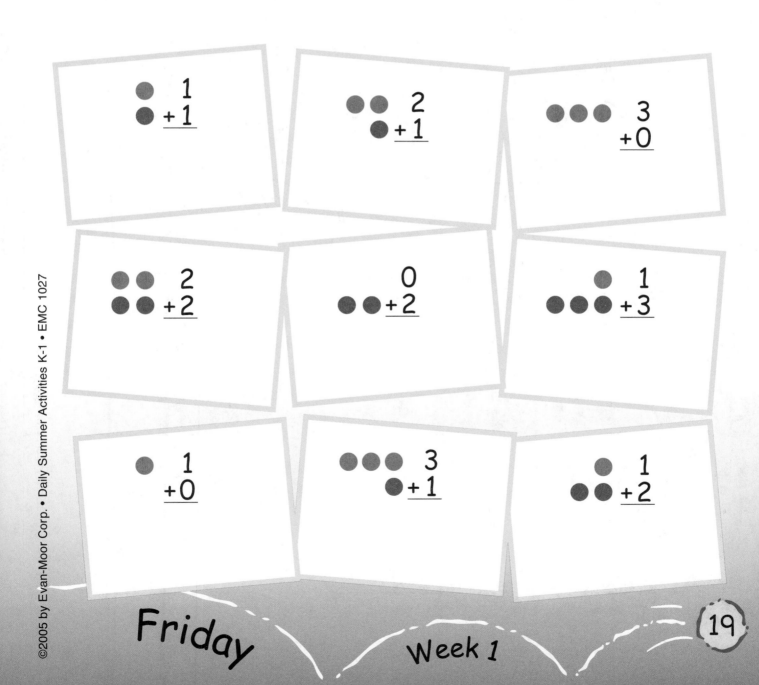

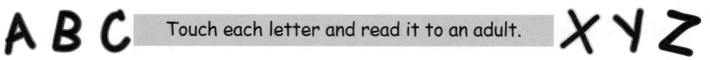

How many animals can you find?

How many divers can you find?

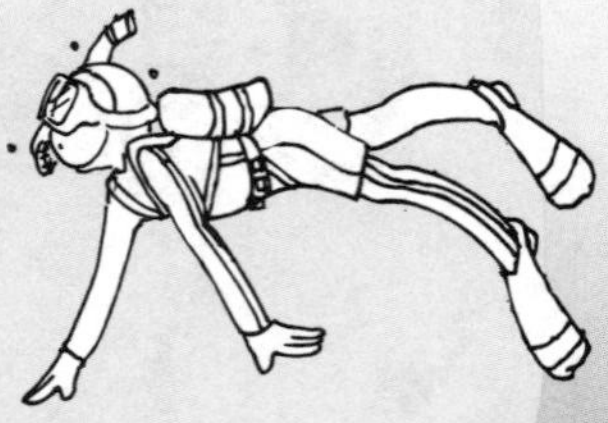

WEEK 2

Color a ☆ for each page finished.

		Parent's Initials
Monday	☆ ☆	________
Tuesday	☆ ☆	________
Wednesday	☆ ☆	________
Thursday	☆ ☆	________
Friday	☆ ☆	________

Spelling Words

cat
dog

What Happened Today? Write about one thing you did each day.

Monday ______________________________

____

____

Tuesday ______________________________

____

____

Wednesday ______________________________

____

____

Thursday ______________________________

____

____

Friday ______________________________

____

____

Keeping Track Color a book for every 10 minutes you read.

Monday	Tuesday	Wednesday	Thursday	Friday

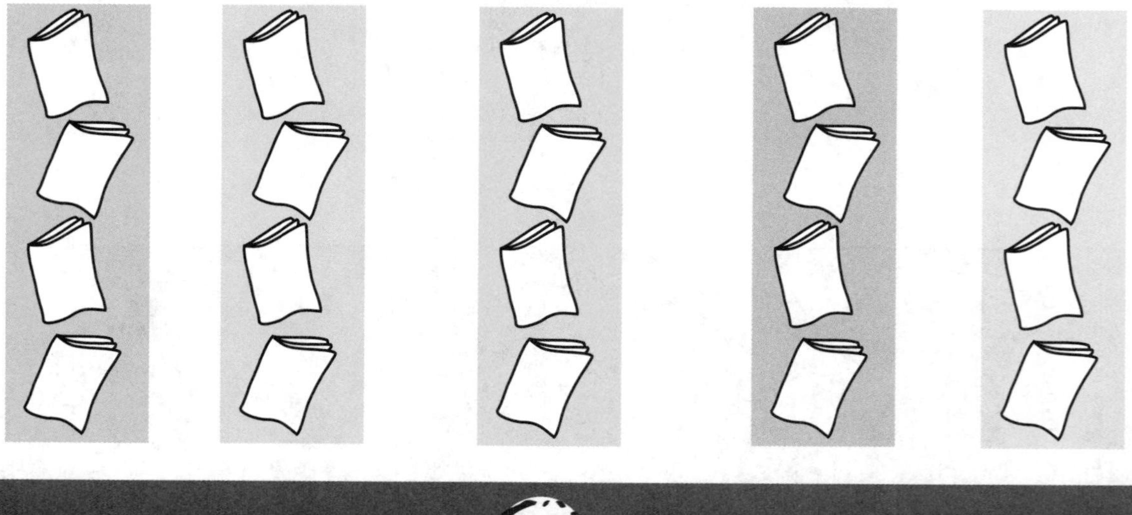

Dd

Trace and Write

d d d D D D

Which pictures begin with the sound made by the letter d? Color them yellow.

Make an **X** on the pictures that **end** with the same sound.

Circle the pictures that are the **same** in each row.

Trace and Write

6 6 6 6

7 7 7 7

8 8 8 8

9 9 9 9

10 10 10 10 10

Count to 20 for an adult. **I can count to 20.** yes no

Week 2 Monday

Spell It!

Practice spelling cat and dog.

Write a letter in each box.

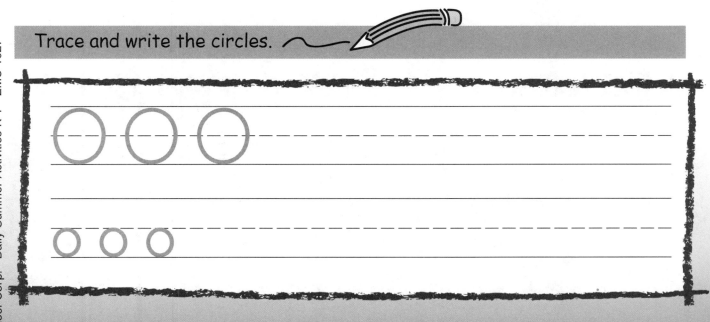

cat dog

Trace and write the words.

cat

dog

Trace and write the circles.

O O O

o o o

Circle the letters that are the **same** in each row.

b	c	b	d	a	b	c	b
c	c	o	c	c	a	c	e
d	h	d	b	g	d	d	b

Color 1.

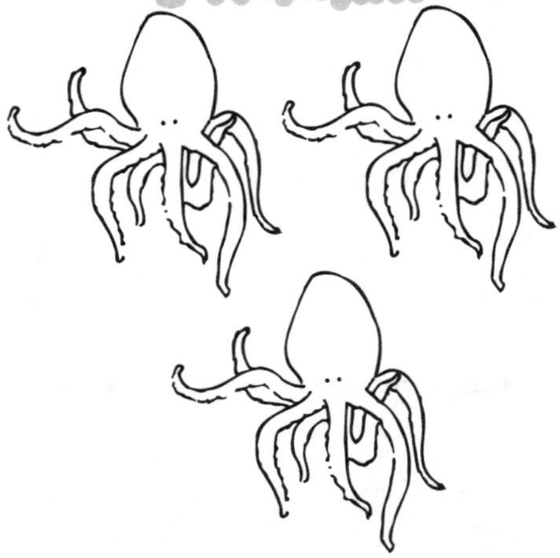

Color 3.

Color 2.

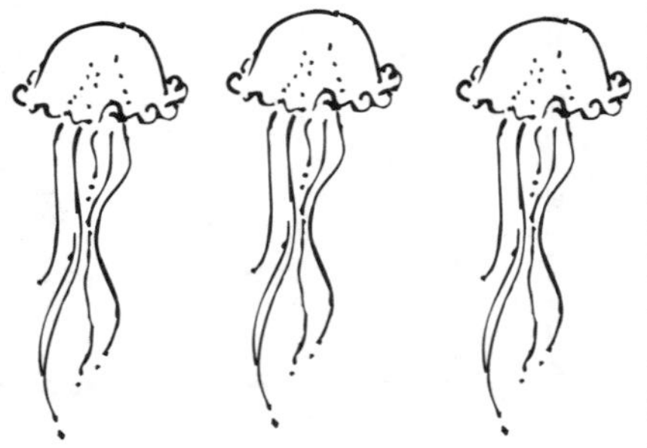

Color 5.

Color 3.

Color 4.

In the Garden

bug 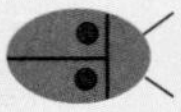

bee 

bird 

Ann can see a bird.

Ted can see a bee.

Pam can see a bug.

I can see me.

What did I see? Match.

Ff

Trace and Write

f ff

F FF

Which pictures begin with the sound made by the letter f?
Color them green.

Trace and color the shapes.

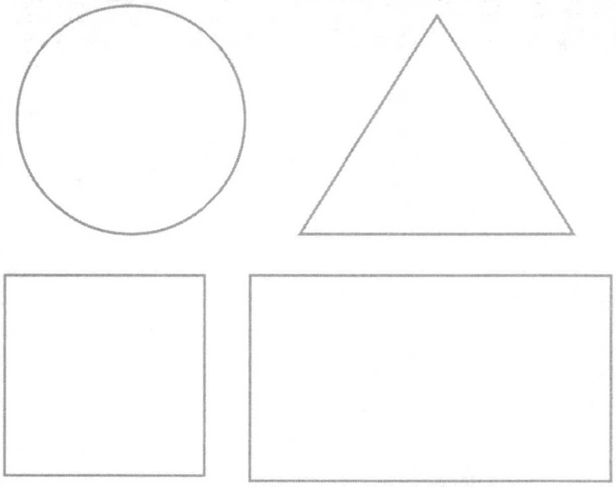

Name the shapes for an adult.

Fill in the missing letters.

a ____ear and a ____ish

Copy the picture and color it the same.

My sailboat can ______________________________ .

WHERE IS IT? Circle the answers.

up | down | in | out

up down

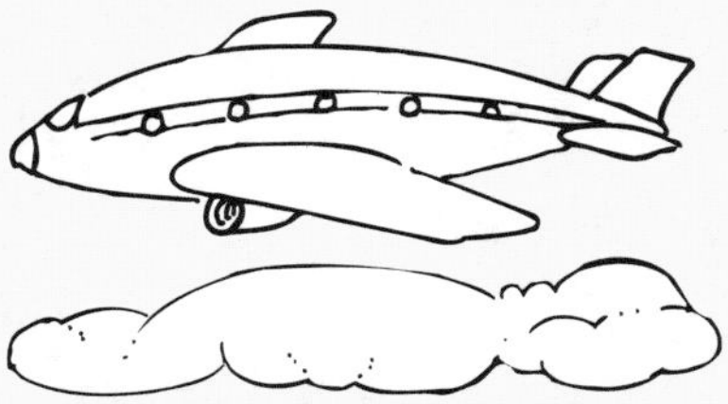

up down

in out

in out

Make an **X** on the pictures that **begin** with the same sound.

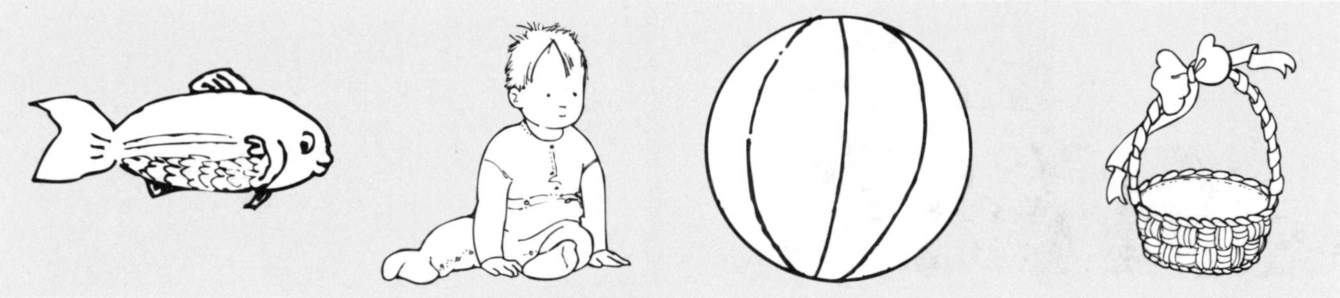

MATH TIME

2 − 1	1 − 1	3 − 2	3 − 0
2 − 2	1 − 0	4 − 1	3 − 3
4 − 2	3 − 1	4 − 3	2 − 0

Match the picture to its beginning sound.

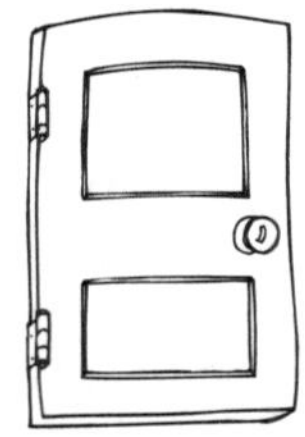

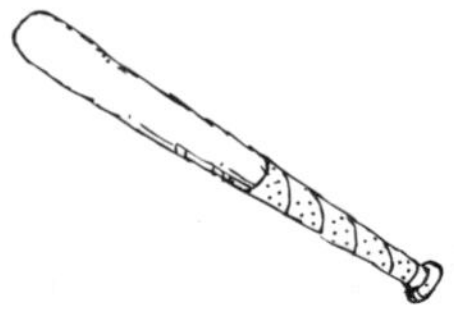

5

b

c

f

d

Color the biggest thing in each row.
Make an X on the smallest thing in each row.

Start at 1 and connect the dots. Color the picture.

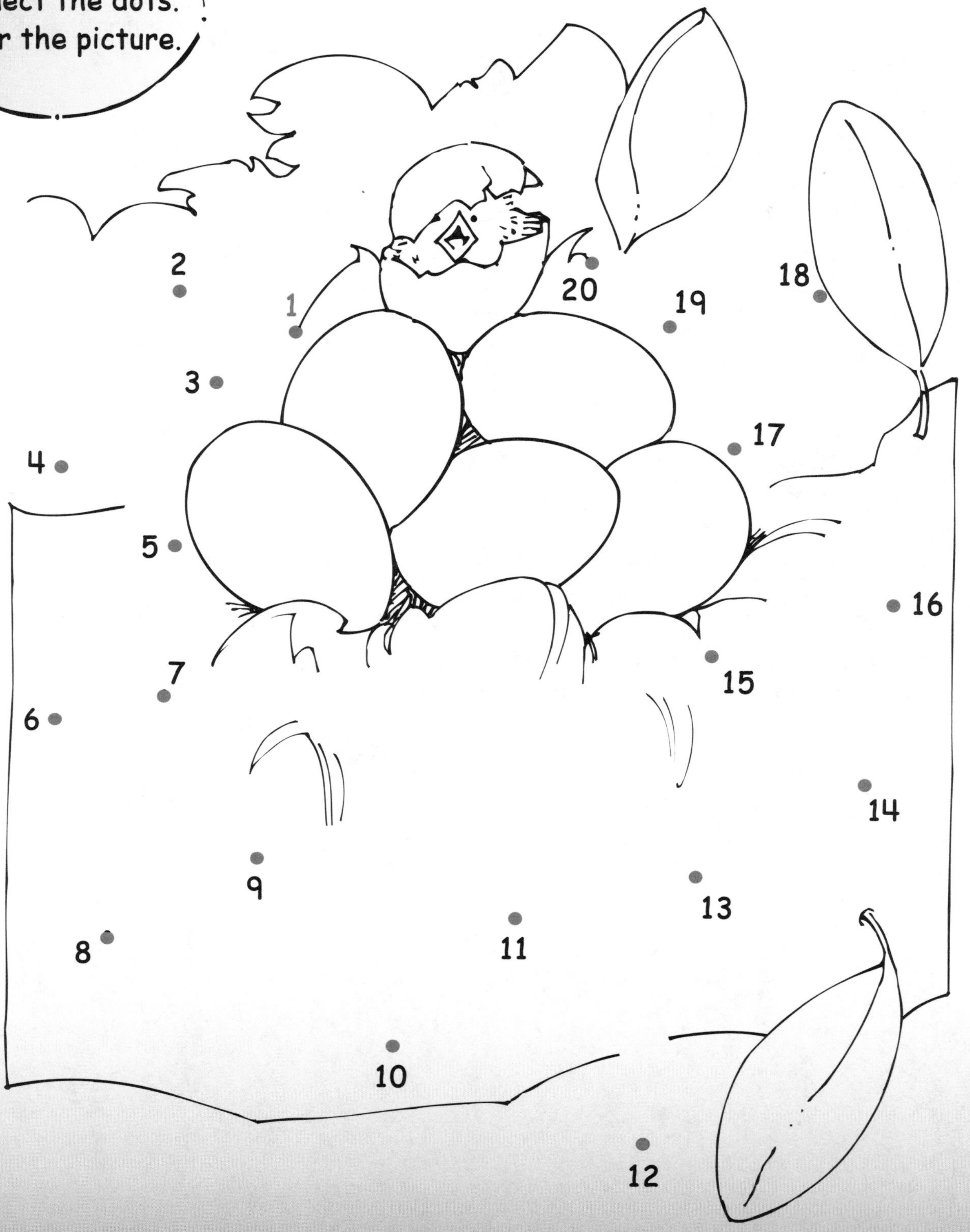

How many eggs have not hatched?________

WEEK 3

Color a ★ for each page finished.

		Parent's Initials
Monday	☆ ☆	________
Tuesday	☆ ☆	________
Wednesday	☆ ☆	________
Thursday	☆ ☆	________
Friday	☆ ☆	________

Spelling Words

yes

no

What Happened Today? Write about one thing you did each day.

Monday ____

____

____

Tuesday ____

____

____

Wednesday ____

____

____

Thursday ____

____

____

Friday ____

____

____

Keeping Track Color a book for every 10 minutes you read.

Monday	Tuesday	Wednesday	Thursday	Friday

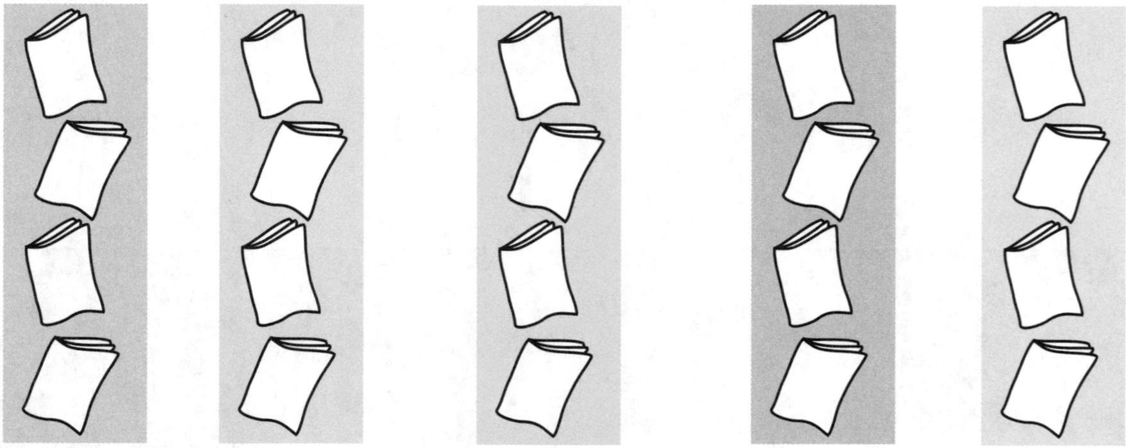

Gg

Trace and Write

g g g G G G

Which pictures begin with the sound made by the letter g?
Color them orange.

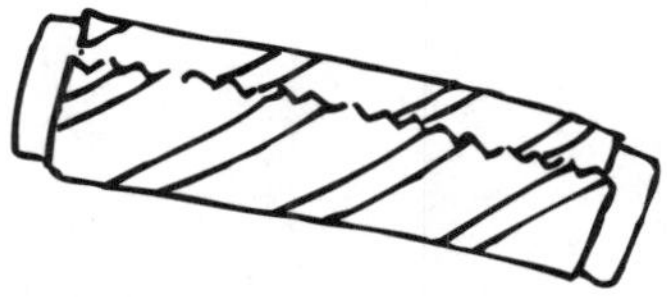

Fill in the missing letters.

____ive ____eese

What Goes Together?

Color plants green and yellow.
Color animals brown and black.

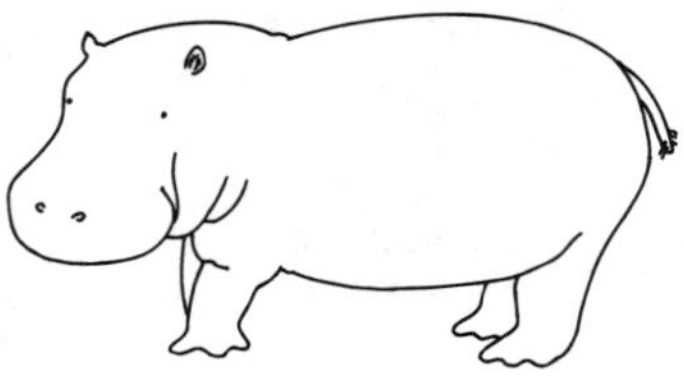

MATH TIME

Trace the numbers.
Fill in the missing numbers.

1 2 3 4 5 6 7 8 9 10

1 ___ 3 ___ 5 ___ 7 ___ 9 ___

___ 2 ___ 4 ___ 6 ___ 8 ___ 10

Count to 30 for an adult. **I can count to 30.** yes no

Spell It!

Practice spelling yes and no.

Write a letter in each box.

yes no

Trace and write the words.

yes

no

Trace and write the letters using your best handwriting.

A E F H I K L M

N T V W X Y Z

Is it REAL or MAKE-BELIEVE?

Circle the set in each row that has **more** objects.

CATS

Cats can run.

Cats can hop.

Cats can jump.

Cats can stop.

Circle the words that rhyme.

1. hop wash shop
2. stop mop jump
3. top run pop

Hh

Trace and Write

h h h H H H

Which pictures begin with the sound made by the letter h?
Color them brown.

MATH TIME

Use counters if you need help.

1 + 1	2 − 1	3 + 0	1 + 2	2 − 2	3 + 1
4 − 1	3 − 2	2 + 1	4 − 2	2 + 2	3 − 1

Draw a duck.
Color it.

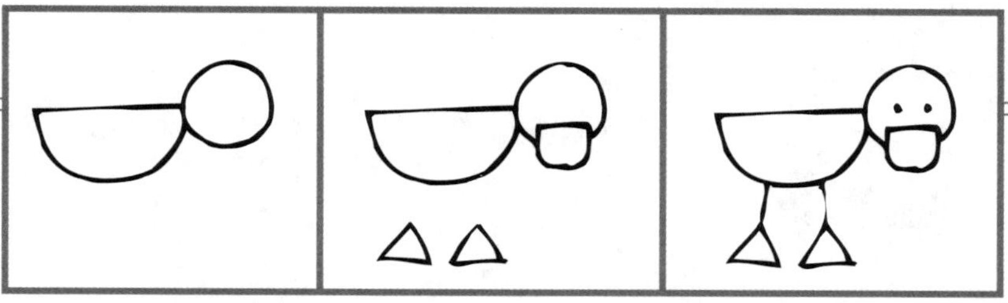

The duck is ______________________________ .

WHERE IS IT?

Find the cat.

over under

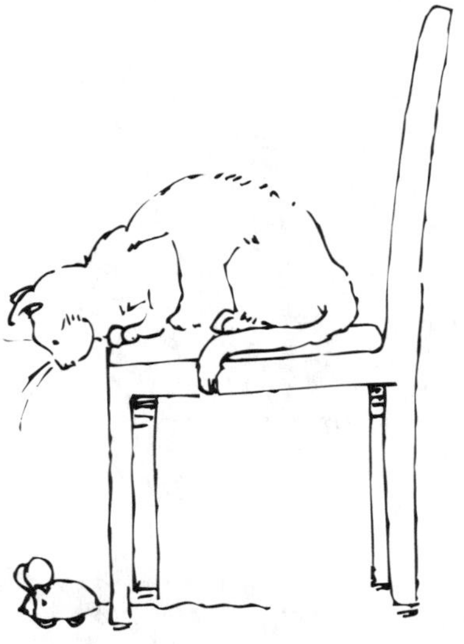

over under

over under

Match.

B	d
C	f
D	b
G	c
F	h
H	g

MATH TIME

How much money is in each bank?

5¢ 10¢ 15¢

5¢ 10¢ 15¢

5¢ 10¢ 15¢

Jj

Trace and Write

j j j   J J J

Color the pictures that begin with the sound made by the letter j.

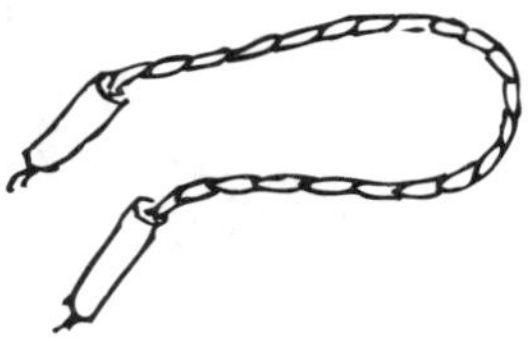

How many do you see?

1 2 3 4 5

1 2 3 4 5

1 2 3 4 5

1 2 3 4 5

1 2 3 4 5

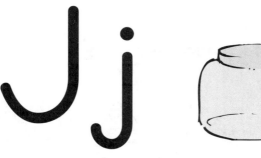

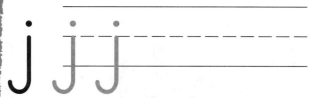

1 2 3 4 5

Start at the mouse.
Draw a line from the mouse to the monkey.
Touch only the animals.

WEEK 4

Color a ★ for each page finished.

		Parent's Initials
Monday	☆ ☆	________
Tuesday	☆ ☆	________
Wednesday	☆ ☆	________
Thursday	☆ ☆	________
Friday	☆ ☆	________

Spelling Words

red

six

What Happened Today? Write about one thing you did each day.

Monday ______________________________

____

____

Tuesday ______________________________

____

____

Wednesday ______________________________

____

____

Thursday ______________________________

____

____

Friday ______________________________

____

____

Keeping Track Color a book for every 10 minutes you read.

Monday Tuesday Wednesday Thursday Friday

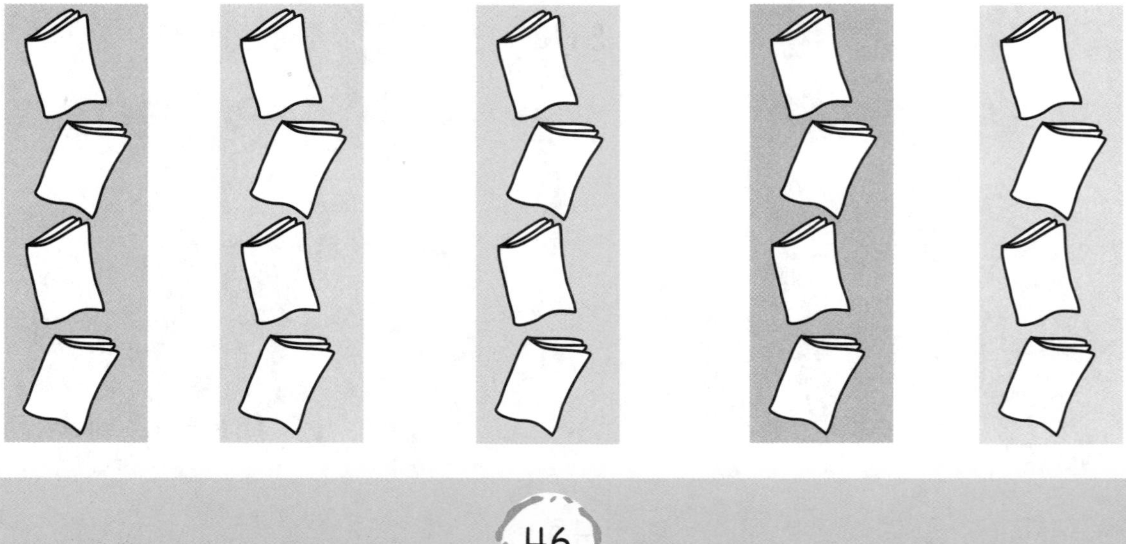

K k

Trace and Write

k k k K K K

Which pictures begin with the sound made by the letter k?
Color them black.

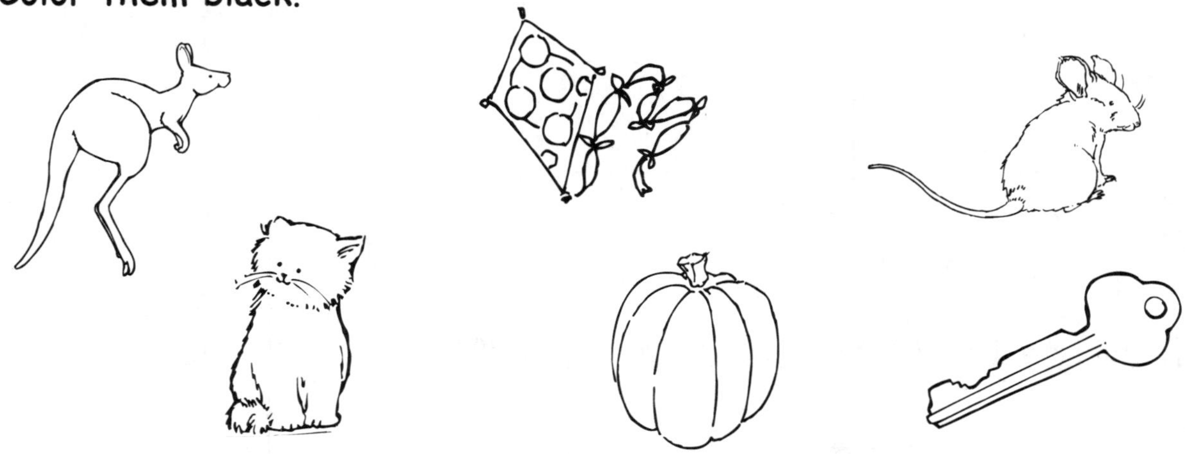

Fill in the missing letters.

a ___itten in a ___ox

Write the beginning and ending sounds.

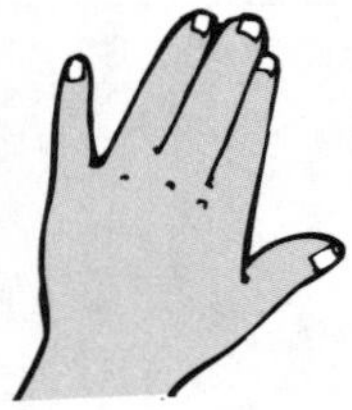

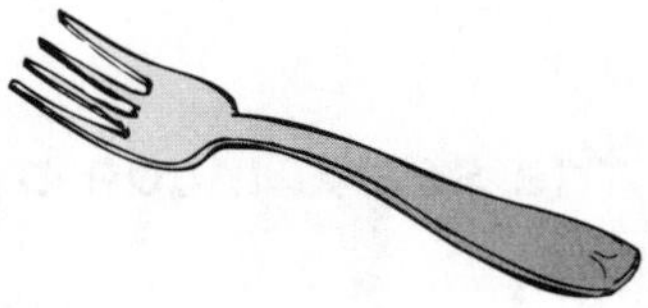

Count from 1 to 10.

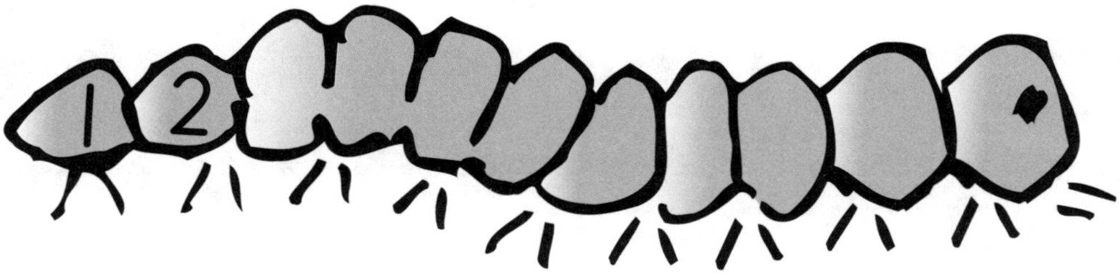

Count from 10 to 1.

Count to 40 for an adult. **I can count to 40.** yes no

Spell It!

Practice spelling red and six.

Write a letter in each box.

red

six

Trace and write the words.

red

six

Trace and write the letters using your best handwriting.

Little Miss Muffet

sat on a tuffet.

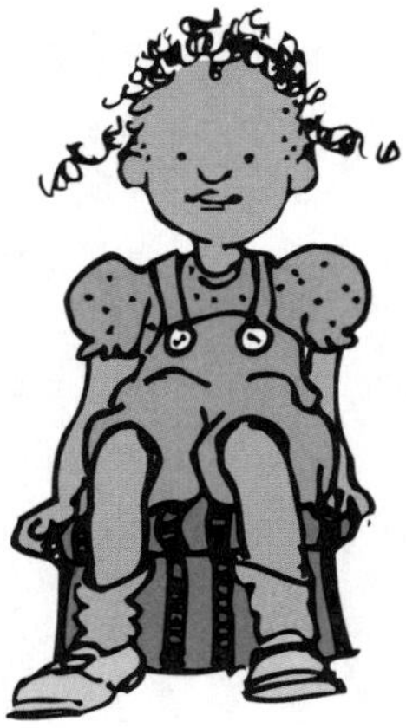

Where will you see it?

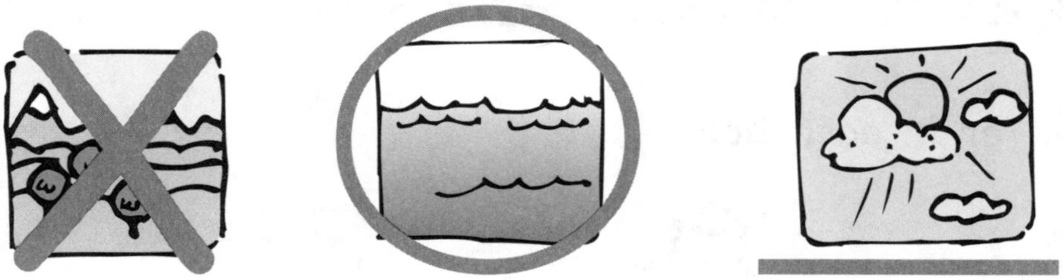

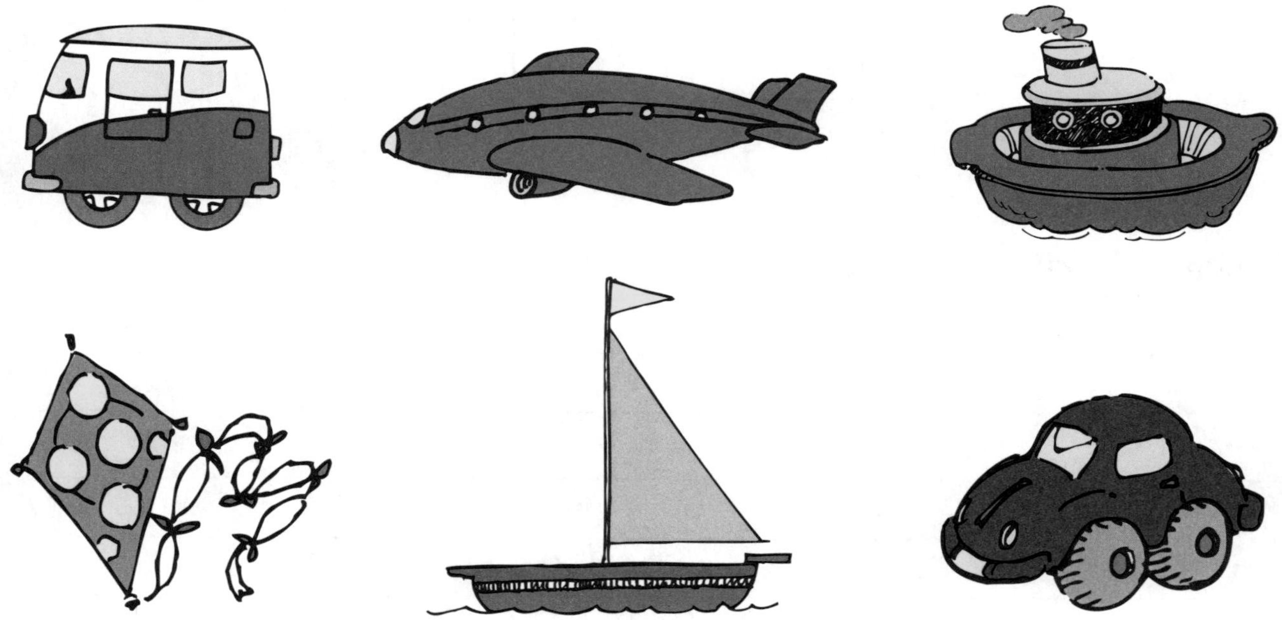

Count and color.

Color 6.	Color 4.	Color 9.
○ ○ ○ ○ ○ ○ ○ ○ ○ ○	○ ○ ○ ○ ○ ○ ○ ○ ○ ○	○ ○ ○ ○ ○ ○ ○ ○ ○ ○
Color 7.	Color 10.	Color 8.
○ ○ ○ ○ ○ ○ ○ ○ ○ ○	○ ○ ○ ○ ○ ○ ○ ○ ○ ○	○ ○ ○ ○ ○ ○ ○ ○ ○ ○

Week 4

Tuesday

©2005 by Evan-Moor Corp. • Daily Summer Activities K-1 • EMC 1027

On My Feet

feet 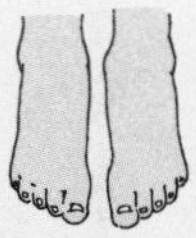

socks 

boots 

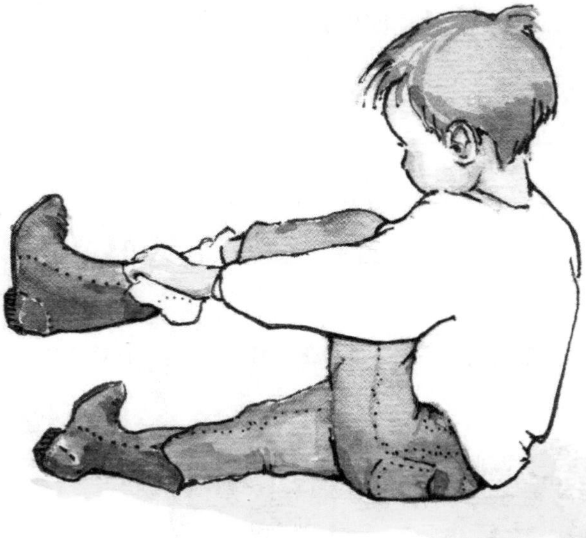

Two feet.

Two socks on my feet.

Two boots on my feet.

Off I go!

Color what you can wear on your feet.

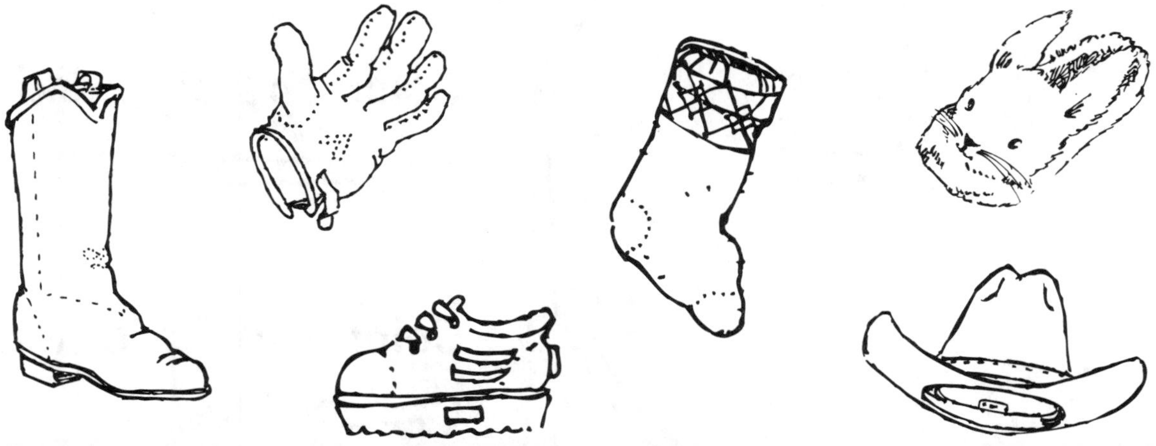

Ll

Trace and Write

l ll L LL

Circle the pictures that begin with the sound made by the letter l.

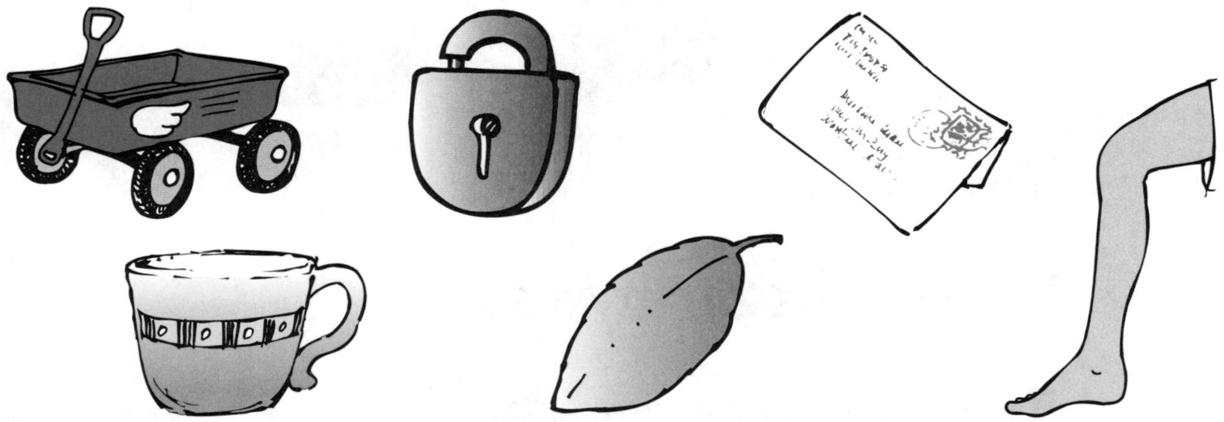

Trace the numbers on the clock .

Color the big hand  green.

Color the little hand  blue.

Draw a wagon.

I carry ______________________ in my wagon.

Make an X on the left hand.
Color the right hand.

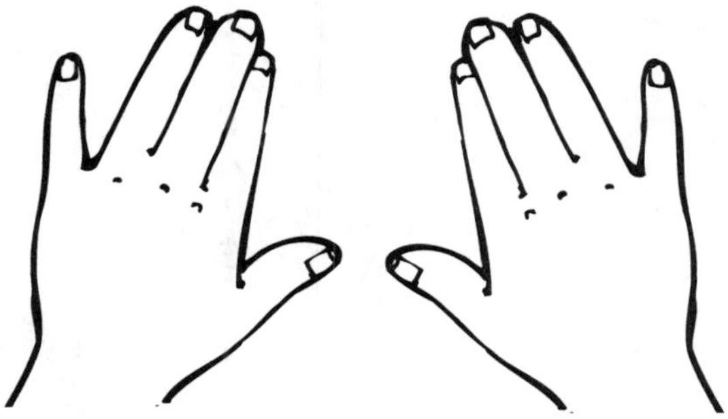

Make an X on the right boot.
Color the left boot.

A B C Fill in the missing letters of the alphabet. X Y Z

A B __ D E __ G H __

J __ __ M N O __ Q __

__ T U __ __ X __ Z

Trace and write the number.

0 0 0

Color the pictures.

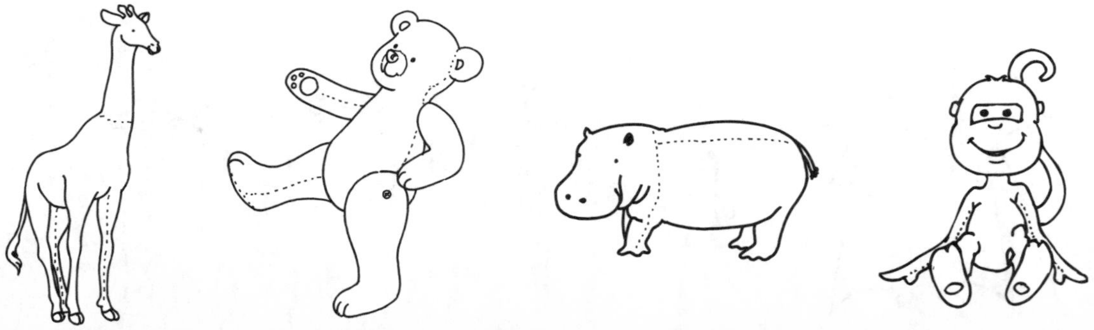

yellow brown black red

How many  do you see? ____

How many  do you see? ____

Mm

Trace and Write

m m m M M M

Make an X on the pictures that begin with the sound made by the letter m.

MATCH THE SHAPES

Draw the other side.
Color it the same.

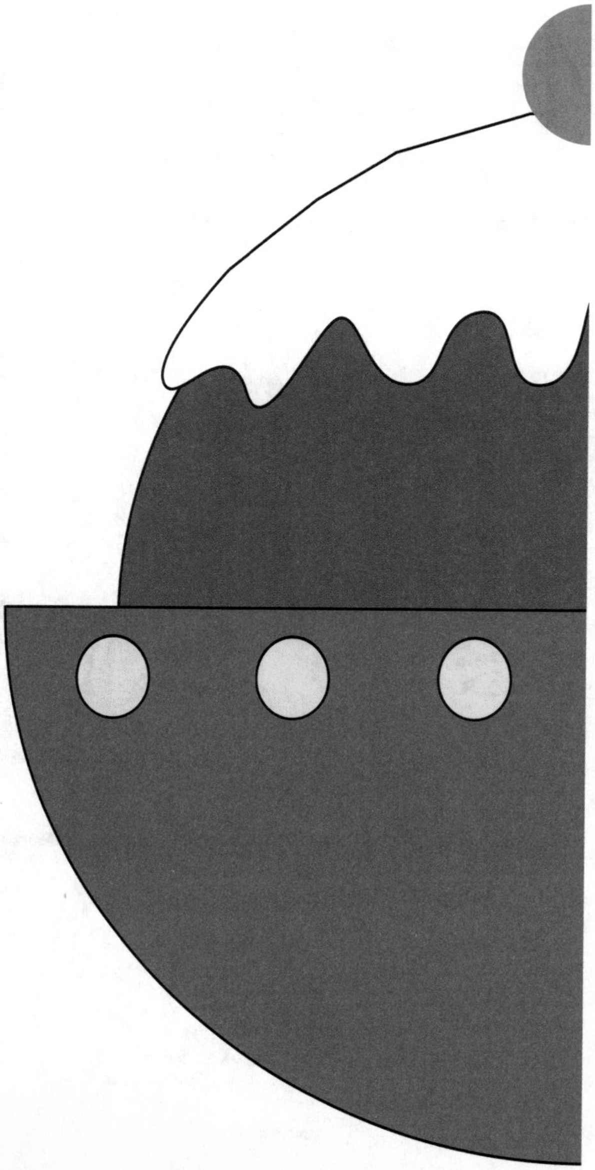

WEEK 5

Color a ☆ for each page finished.

		Parent's Initials
Monday	☆ ☆	________
Tuesday	☆ ☆	________
Wednesday	☆ ☆	________
Thursday	☆ ☆	________
Friday	☆ ☆	________

Spelling Words

run

jump

What Happened Today? Write about one thing you did each day.

Monday ____________________

____

____

Tuesday ____________________

____

____

Wednesday ____________________

____

____

Thursday ____________________

____

____

Friday ____________________

____

____

Keeping Track Color a book for every 10 minutes you read.

Monday	Tuesday	Wednesday	Thursday	Friday

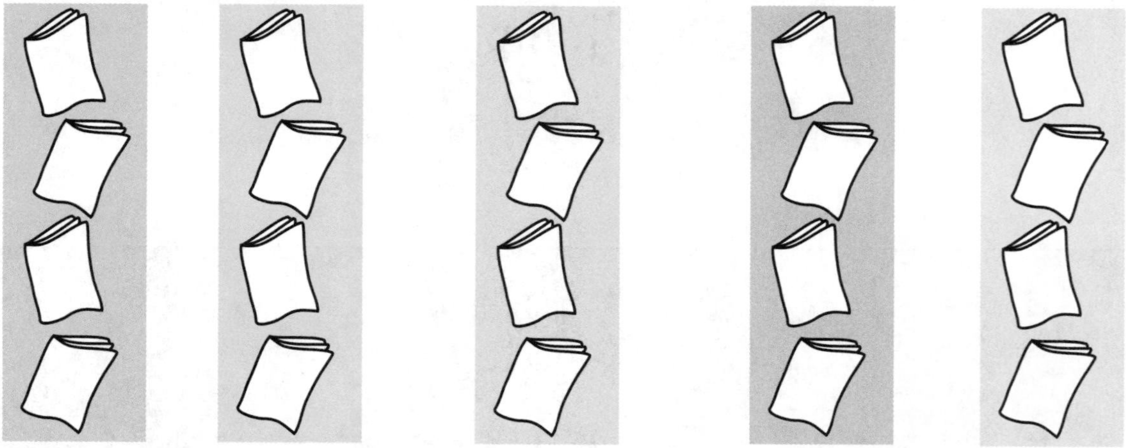

Nn

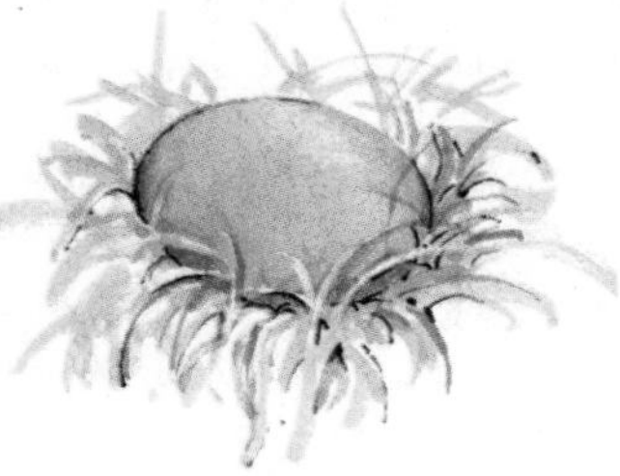

Trace and Write

n n n ____________ N N N ____________

Circle the pictures that begin with the sound made by the letter n.

Fill in the missing letters.

a ____og in a ____oat

____uts in a ____ox

Circle the letters that go together.

g	G	D	C
h	W	M	H
j	G	Q	J
n	M	N	Z

k	S	K	T
l	L	T	I
m	N	W	M
b	B	D	C

123 Fill in the missing numbers. 456

1 2 3 4 5 6 7 8 9 10

1 __2__ 3   2 ____ 4   6 ____ 8

5 ____ 7   3 ____ 5   8 ____ 10

7 ____ 9   4 ____ 6   9 ____ 11

Count to 50 for an adult. **I can count to 50.** yes no

Spell It!

Practice spelling run and jump.

Write a letter in each box.

run jump

Trace and write the words.

run

jump

Trace and write the letters using your best handwriting.

Humpty Dumpty

sat on a wall.

Match the pictures that are opposites.

Draw dots on the clown hats.

Where Is Pup?

here is
Here Is

Is Pup here?

Pup is not here.

Is Pup here?

Pup is not here.

Here is Pup!

Was Pup here?

yes no

yes no

yes no

Pp

Trace and Write

p p p   P P P

Make an X on the pictures that begin with the sound made by the letter p.

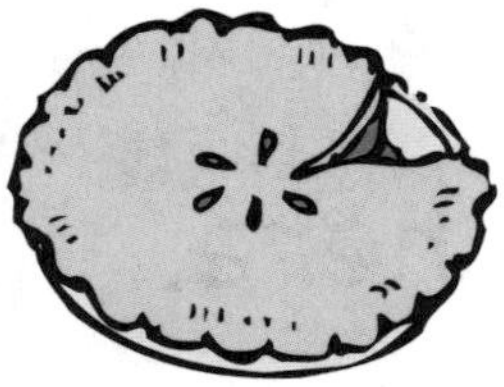

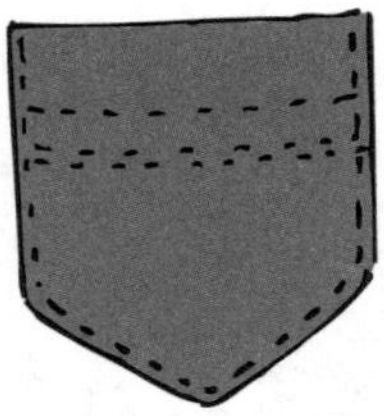

Circle the set in each row that has the **least** number of objects.

Draw a cat.
Color it.

My cat is ______________________________ .

Circle the pictures.

What is **up**?

What is **down**?

What is **left**?

Match the pictures that rhyme.

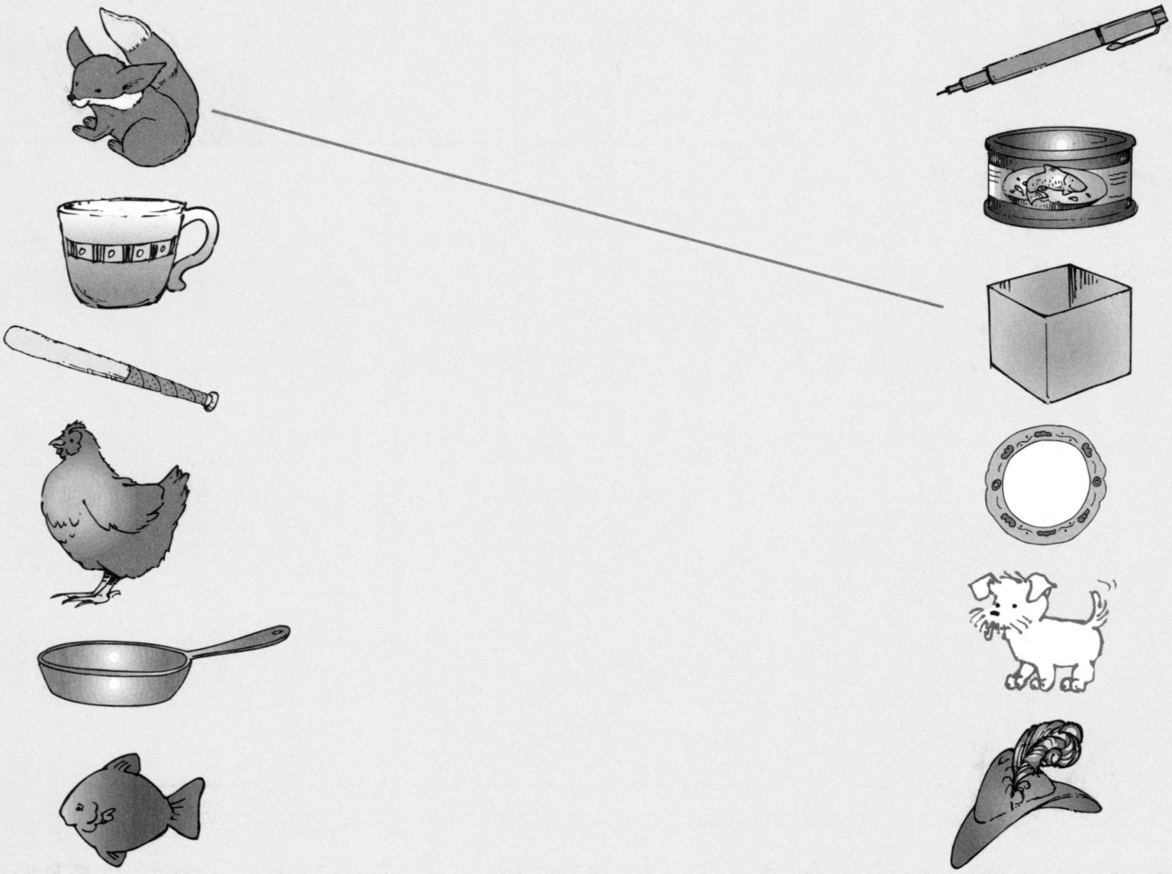

MATH TIME

2 + 1	3 + 3	4 + 1	3 + 2
3 + 1	1 + 4	2 + 4	2 + 2
5 + 0	2 + 3	1 + 3	4 + 2

Qq

Trace and Write

q q q   Q Q Q

Color the pictures that begin with the sound made by the letter q.

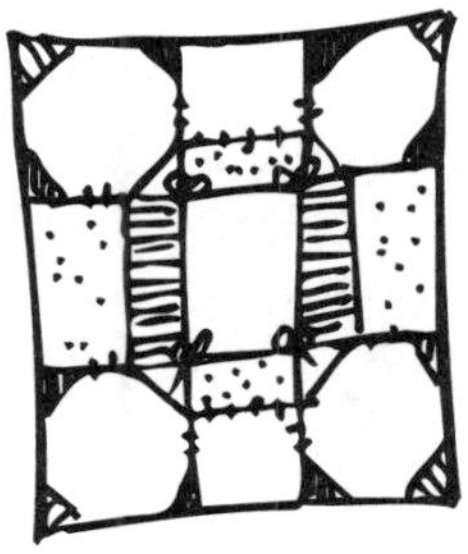

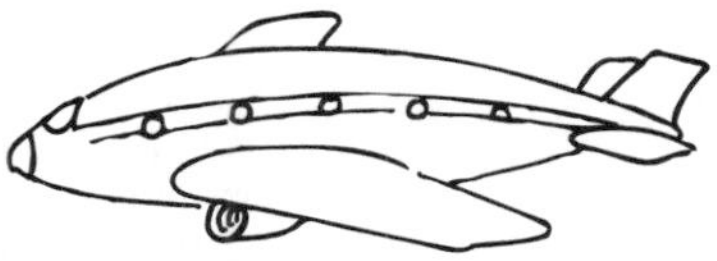

MATH TIME

Trace the numbers to count by 5s.

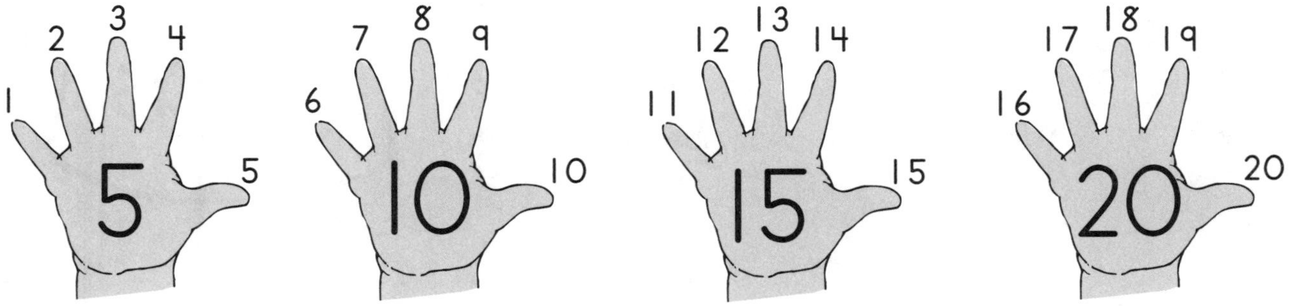

Count by 5s for an adult.

I can count by 5s to 20. yes no

Start at A and connect the dots.
Color the picture.

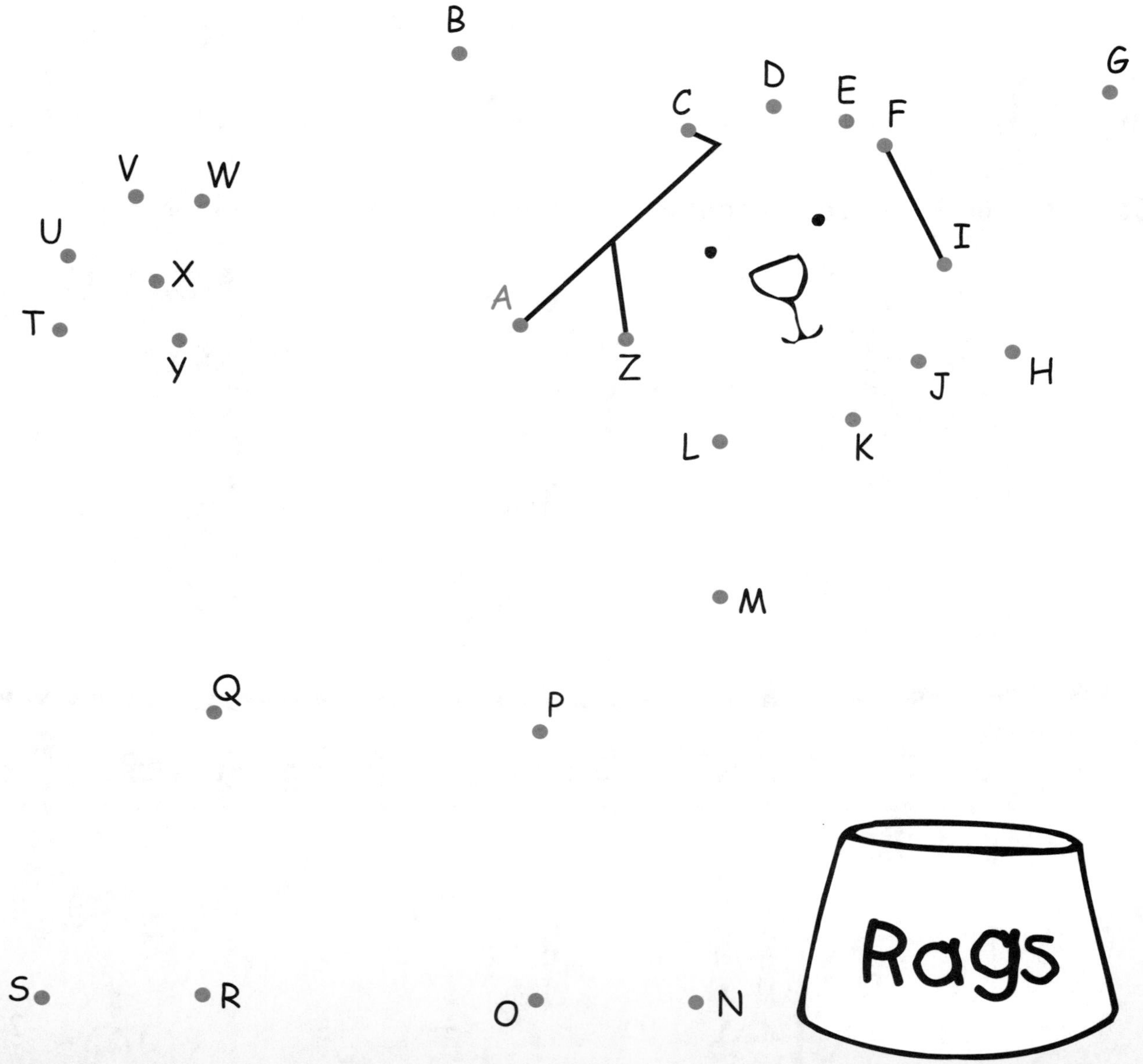

WEEK 6

Color a ☆ for each page finished.

		Parent's Initials
Monday	☆ ☆	________
Tuesday	☆ ☆	________
Wednesday	☆ ☆	________
Thursday	☆ ☆	________
Friday	☆ ☆	________

Spelling Words

see

can

What Happened Today? Write about one thing you did each day.

Monday ____

____

____

Tuesday ____

____

____

Wednesday ____

____

____

Thursday ____

____

____

Friday ____

____

____

Keeping Track Color a book for every 10 minutes you read.

Monday	Tuesday	Wednesday	Thursday	Friday

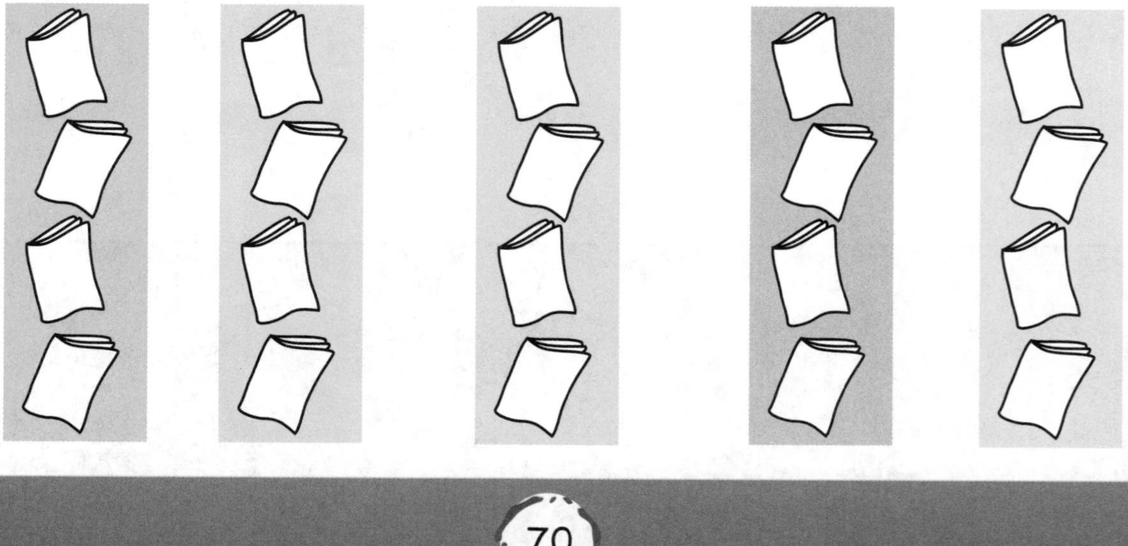

Rr 

Trace and Write

r r r R R R

Color the pictures that begin with the sound made by the letter r.

Fill in the missing letters.

the ____ueen had a ____uilt ☆ a ____obot had a ____og

Circle the ending sound.

b d h

m n r

t d k

g c p

b t k

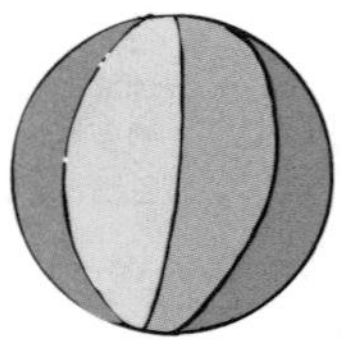
h t l

g k p

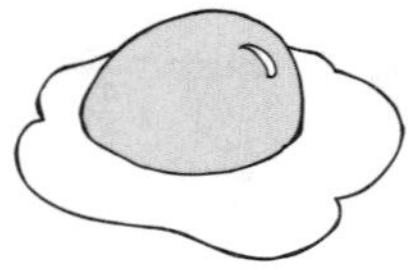
p g d

k t d

z c s

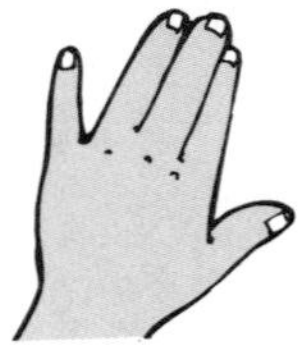
p d b

q g p

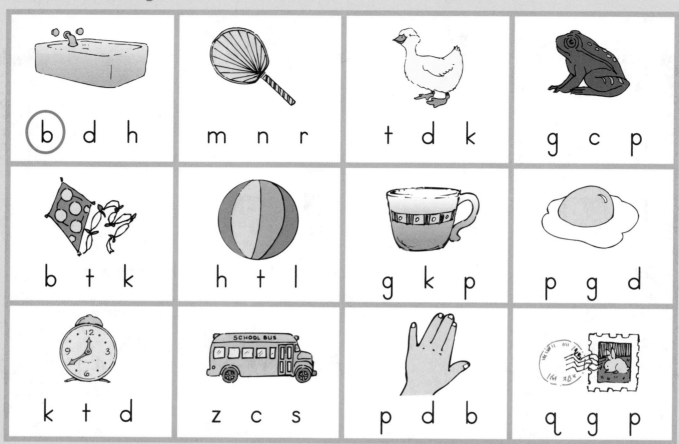

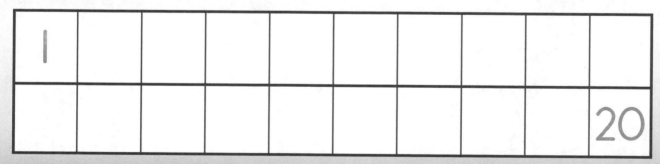

MATH TIME

Touch the numbers and read them.

1 2 3 4 5 6 7 8 9 10

11 12 13 14 15 16 17 18 19 20

Write the numbers 1 to 20.

1									
									20

Count to 60 for an adult. I can count to 60. yes no

Spell It!

Practice spelling see and can.

Write a letter in each box.

see

can

Trace and write the words.

see

can

Copy the sentence using your best handwriting.

Little Bo Peep

has lost her sheep.

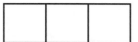

ABC Touch each letter and read it to an adult. XYZ

B	E	Z	A	H	V	J
N	W	M	R	P	C	D
F	Q	X	S	I	U	L
G	K	Y	O	T		

I can read ☐ letters of the alphabet.

What number comes next?

5 6	9 ____	7 ____
15 16	19 ____	17 ____
3 ____	1 ____	6 ____
13 ____	11 ____	16 ____
4 ____	2 ____	8 ____
14 ____	12 ____	18 ____

Where Are the Chickens?

chicken  nest 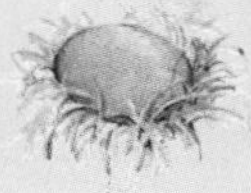 roost 

One chicken on a nest.

Two chickens on the roost.

Three chickens in the pen.

How many chickens?

on the roost ________

in the pen ________

on a nest ________

Ss

Trace and Write

s s s   S S S

Color the pictures that begin with the sound made by the letter s.

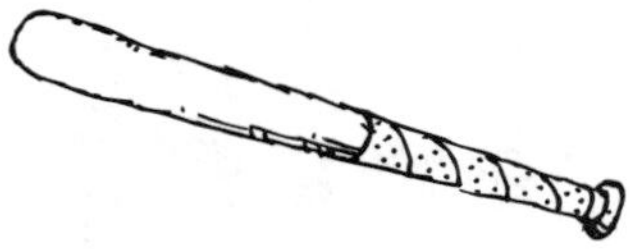

Make an **X** on the set in each row that has **the most** objects.
Circle the set in each row that has **the least** objects.

This is me

I can ____

____.

Count the boxes to tell where the pictures are.

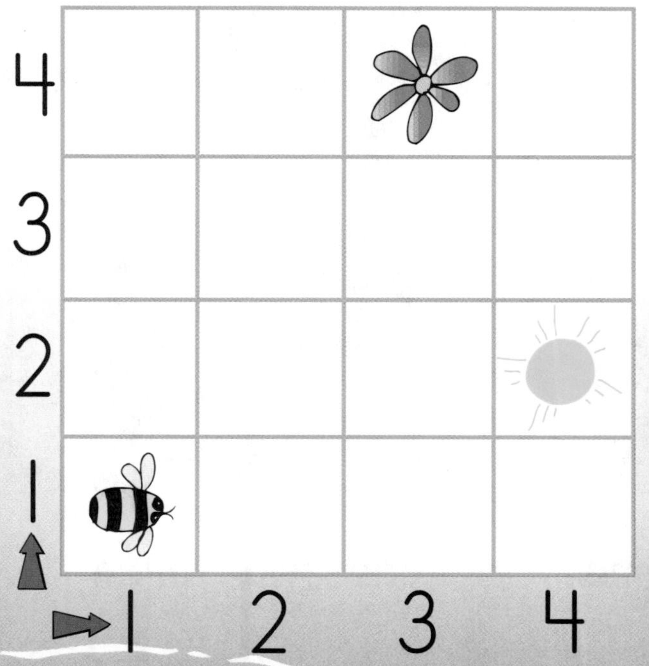

over ➡ up ⬆

1.  over ______ boxes

up ______ boxes

2.  over ______ boxes

up ______ boxes

3.  over ______ box

up ______ box

Draw 5 things in your bedroom.

How many do you see?

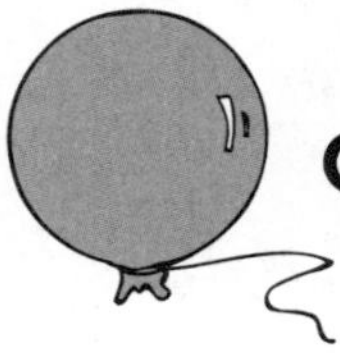
one

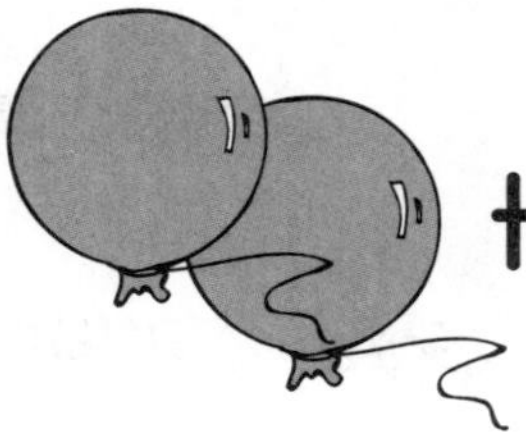
two

three

one two three

one two three

one two three

Aa

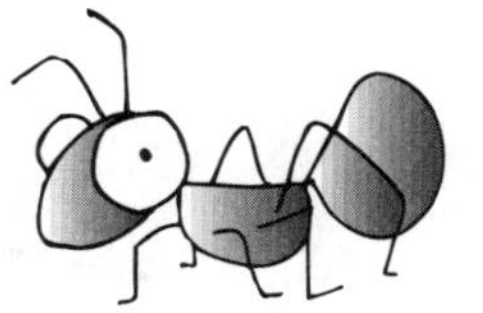

Trace and Write

a a a

A A A

Fill in the missing letter.

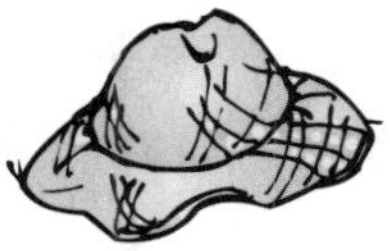

h____t

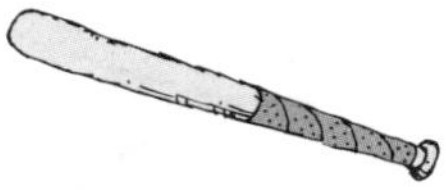

b____t

c____t

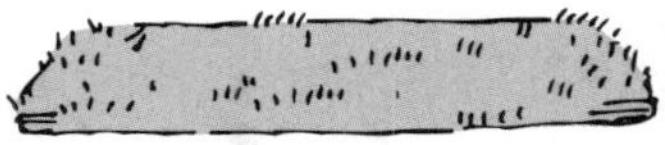

m____t

c____n

____nt

MATH TIME

$5 - 1$

$6 - 2$

$6 - 4$

$5 - 3$

$5 - 4$

$5 - 2$

$6 - 3$

$3 - 2$

Start at a and connect the dots.

I am a ______________________________.

WEEK 7

Color a ☆ for each page finished.

		Parent's Initials
Monday	☆ ☆	________
Tuesday	☆ ☆	________
Wednesday	☆ ☆	________
Thursday	☆ ☆	________
Friday	☆ ☆	________

Spelling Words

is
fast

What Happened Today? Write about one thing you did each day.

Monday ______________________________

____

____

Tuesday ______________________________

____

____

Wednesday ______________________________

____

____

Thursday ______________________________

____

____

Friday ______________________________

____

____

Keeping Track Color a book for every 10 minutes you read.

Monday	Tuesday	Wednesday	Thursday	Friday

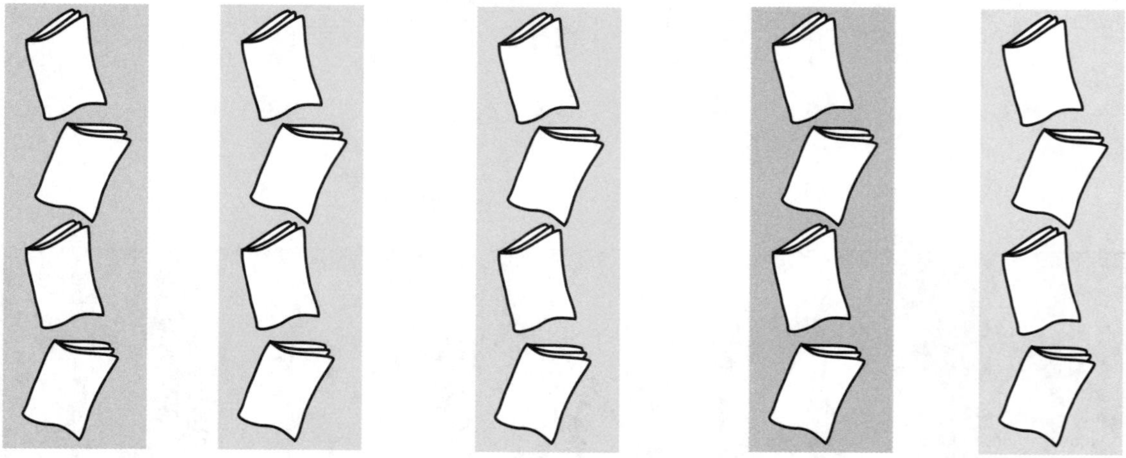

T t

Trace and Write

t t t

T T T

Circle the pictures that begin with the sound made by the letter t.

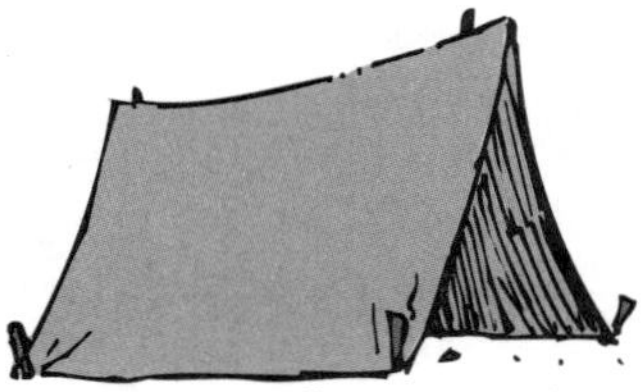

Fill in the missing letters.

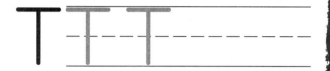

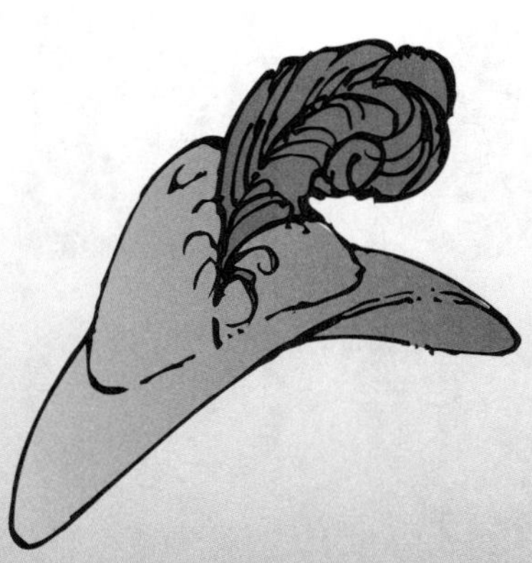

____iger in a ____ent

____eather on a ____at

Color the pictures with the sound of a in ant.

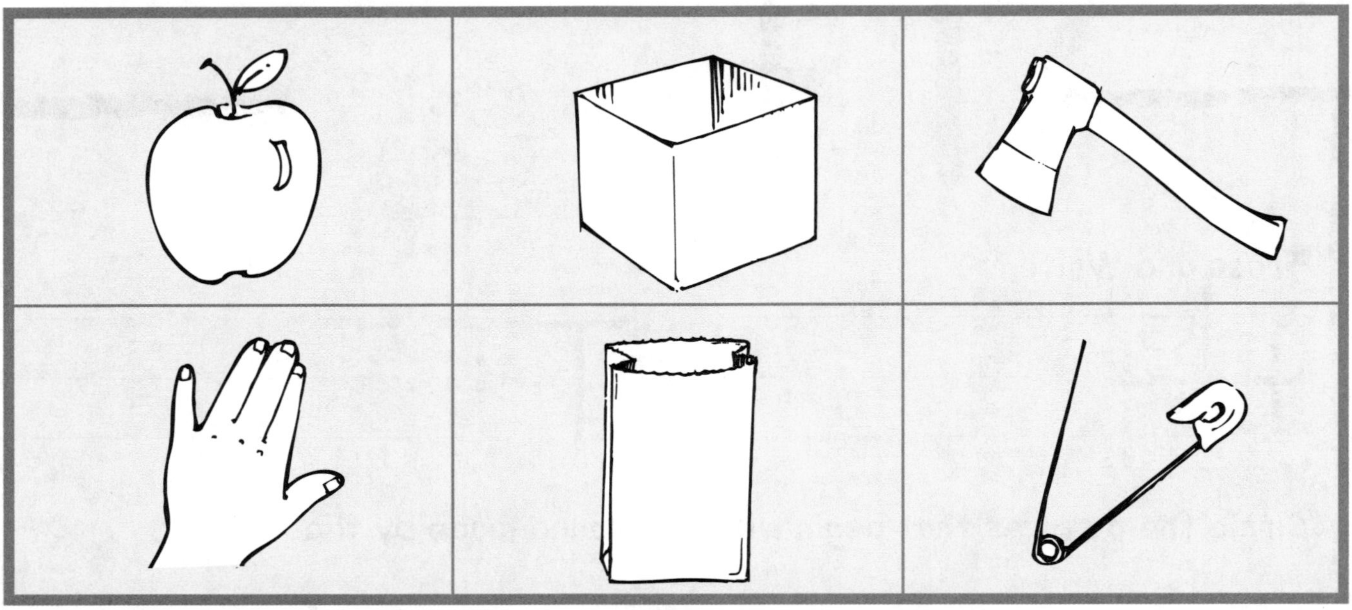

Read these words to an adult.

at	pat	cat	fat	mat	sat
an	can	man	ran	fan	van
bad	had	dad	lad	mad	sad

Complete the patterns.

Count to 70 for an adult. **I can count to 70.** yes no

Spell It!

Practice spelling is and fast.

Write a letter in each box.

is fast

Trace and write the words.

is

fast

Copy the sentence using your best handwriting.

The cow jumped over the moon.

Tuesday

Week 7

Match the pictures to their **beginning** sounds.
Match the lowercase letters to their **capital** letters.

S	r
P	t
T	q
Q	p
R	s

Draw the correct number of petals.

Sam's Van

Sam has a van.

It is big and tan.

The van can go fast.

Sam and his cat get in the van.

Off Sam and the cat go.

Read and draw.

1. a hill
2. a tan van on the hill
3. a boy and a cat in the van

V v

Trace and Write

v v v

V V V

Color the pictures that begin with the sound made by the letter v.

WHAT TIME IS IT?

Tell the time to an adult.

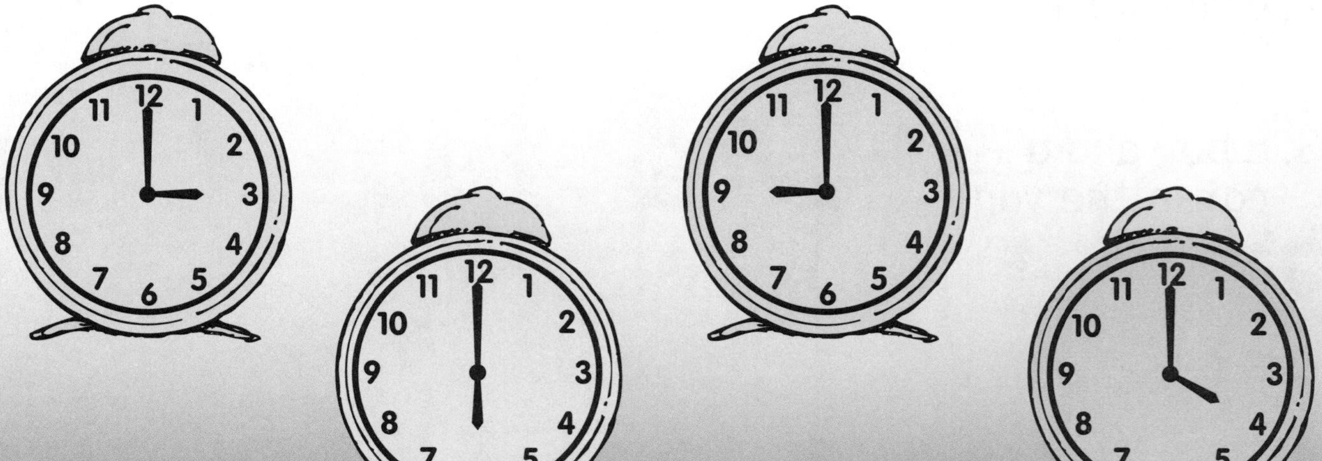

Draw your best friend.

Write about what you and your friend like to do together.

____

____.

Help the rabbit find the carrots.

Write the beginning and ending sounds you hear.

______ ______

______ ______

______ ______

______ ______

______ ______

______ ______

______ ______

______ ______

______ ______

Draw  in the jar.

one blue   **two** black
two green   **three** orange
three red   **one** purple

How many 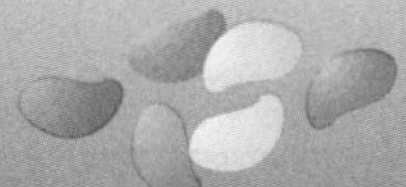 are in the jar? ________

Ee

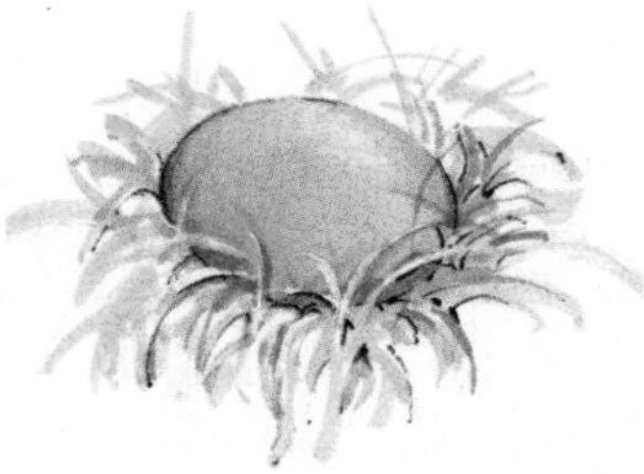

Trace and Write

e e e

E E E

Fill in the missing letter.

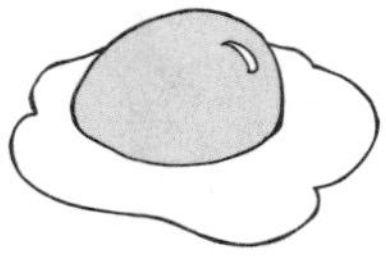

___gg

h___n

10

t___n

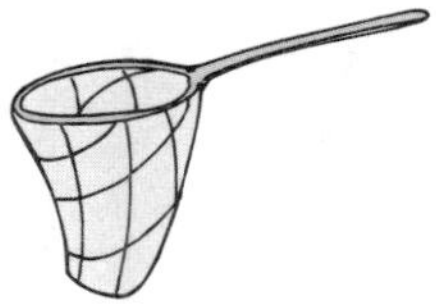

n___t

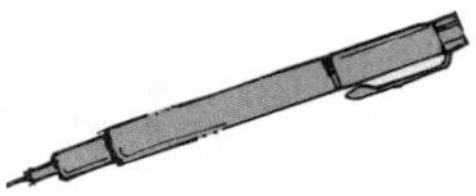

p___n

___lf

MATH TIME

Use counters if you need help.

4	2	4	5	3	6
- 1	+ 4	+ 1	- 3	+ 3	- 2

3	6	2	6	4	2
+ 2	- 4	+ 2	+ 1	- 2	+ 3

Connect the dots. Color the shapes.
Name the shapes to an adult.

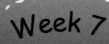

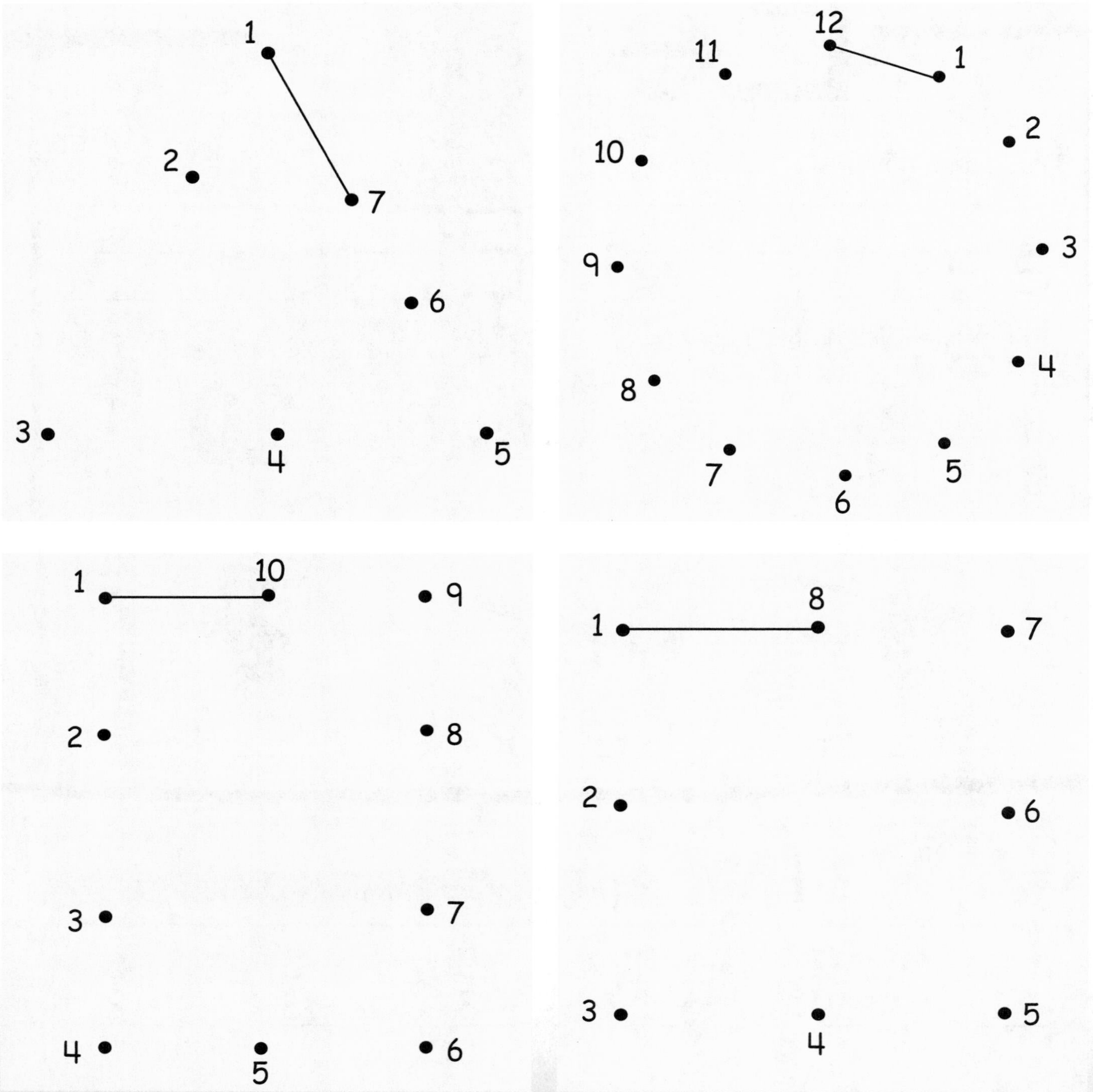

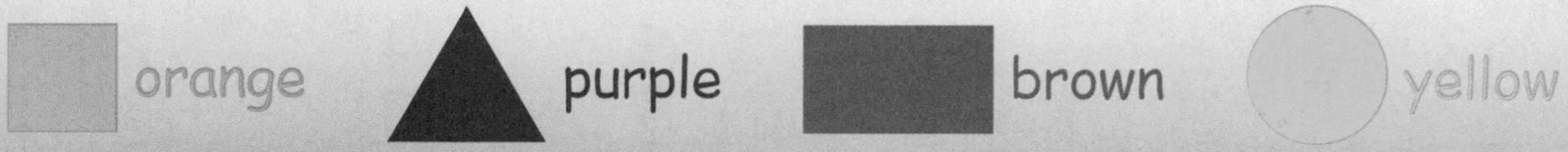

WEEK 8

Color a ★ for each page finished.

		Parent's Initials
Monday	☆ ☆	________
Tuesday	☆ ☆	________
Wednesday	☆ ☆	________
Thursday	☆ ☆	________
Friday	☆ ☆	________

Spelling Words

in

by

What Happened Today? Write about one thing you did each day.

Monday ______________________________

____

____

Tuesday ______________________________

____

____

Wednesday ______________________________

____

____

Thursday ______________________________

____

____

Friday ______________________________

____

____

Keeping Track Color a book for every 10 minutes you read.

Monday	Tuesday	Wednesday	Thursday	Friday

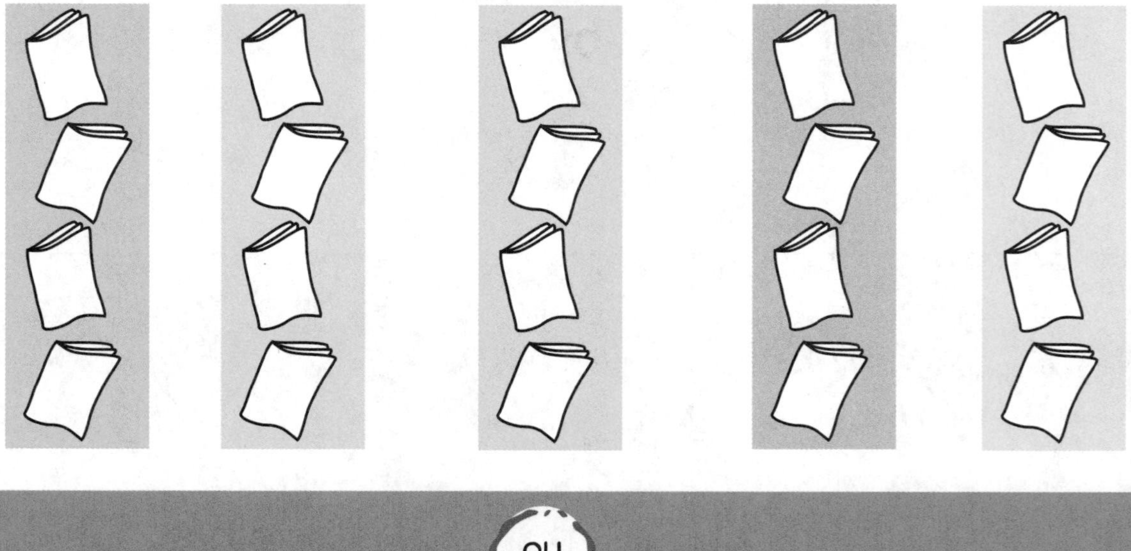

Ww

Trace and Write

w w w

W W W

Which pictures begin with the sound made by the letter w?
Color them red and green.

Fill in the missing letters.

____alls in a ____agon

a ____orm on a ____atermelon

Color the pictures that have the sound of e in ten.

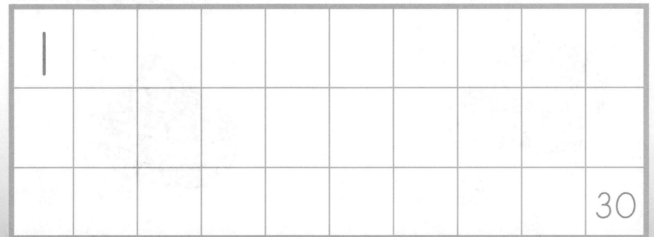

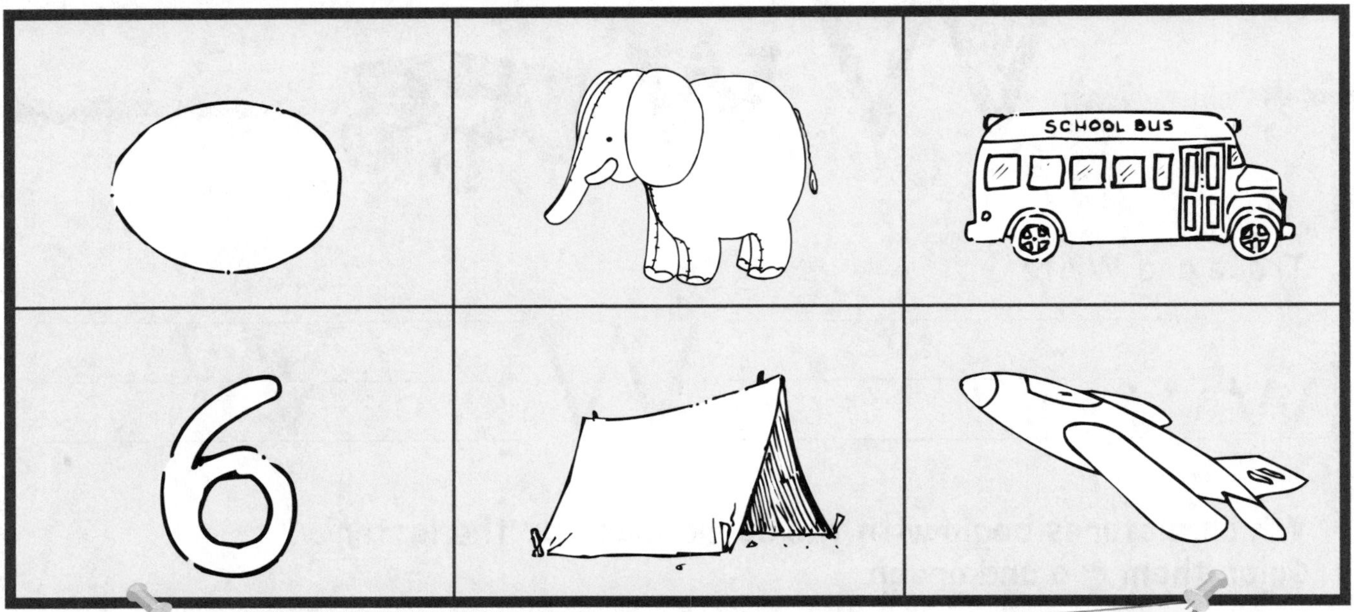

Read these words to an adult.

den	hen	men	pen	ten	Ben
get	let	bet	pet	wet	let
tent	bent	went	sent	dent	Kent

Write the numbers to 30.

1									
									30

Count to 80 for an adult. **I can count to 80.** yes no

Spell It!

Practice spelling in and by.

Write a letter in each box.

in   by

Trace and write the words.

in

by

Trace and write the letters of the alphabet.

a b c d e f g h i j k l m

n o p q r s t u v w x y z

Match the capital and lowercase letters.

A	f
D	b
H	a
F	q
B	d
Q	h

G	j
K	r
J	m
R	e
M	g
E	k

How many do you see?

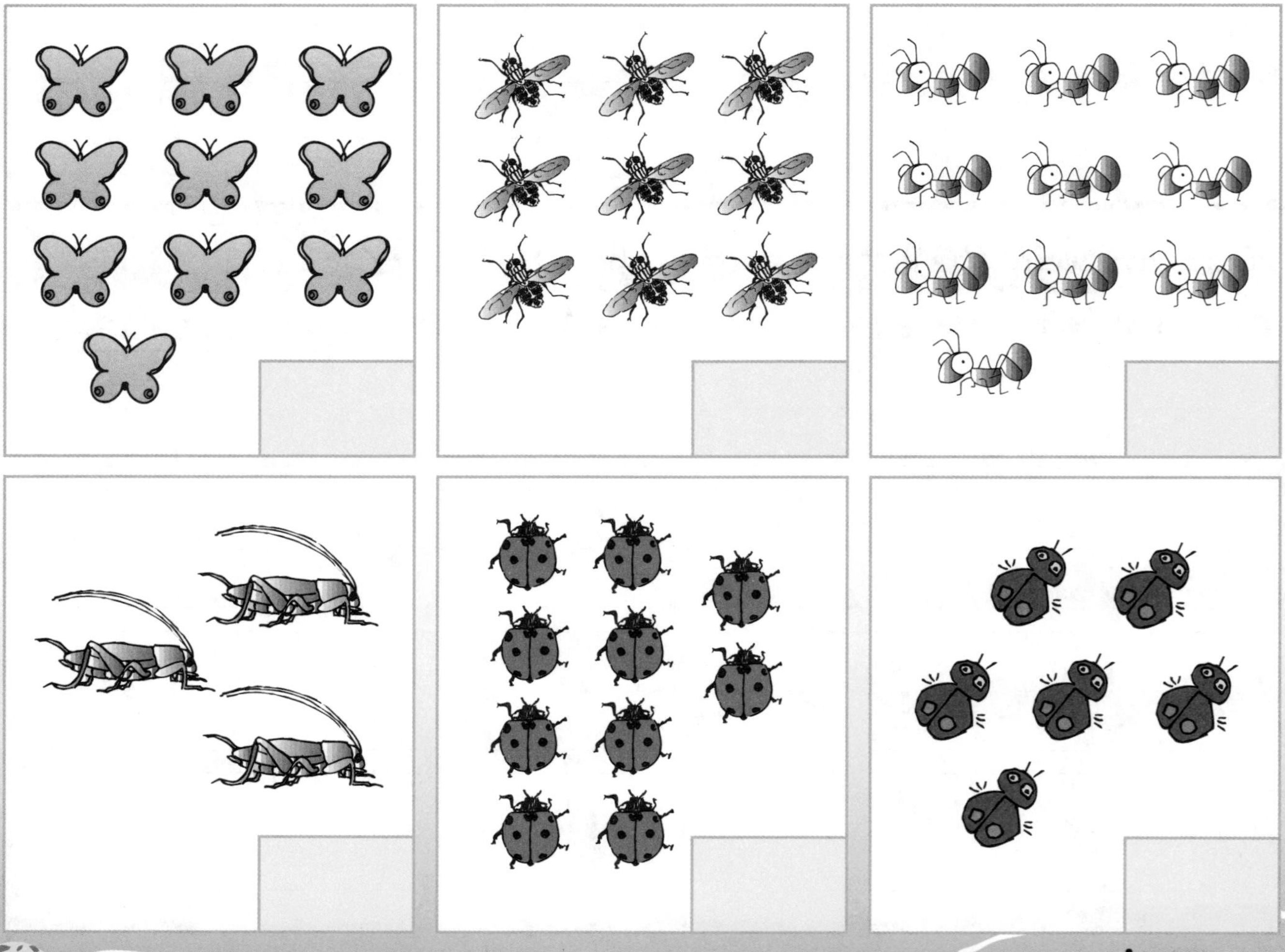

Nap Time

Pig in a pen.

Hen on a nest.

Ted in his bed.

It is time to rest.

Match.

Hen	bed
Ted	pen
Pig	nest

What time is it? Circle the answer.

time to swim

time to dig

time to rest

X x

Trace and Write

x x x

X X X

Circle the pictures that end with the sound made by the letter x.

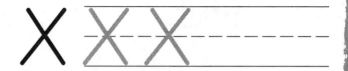

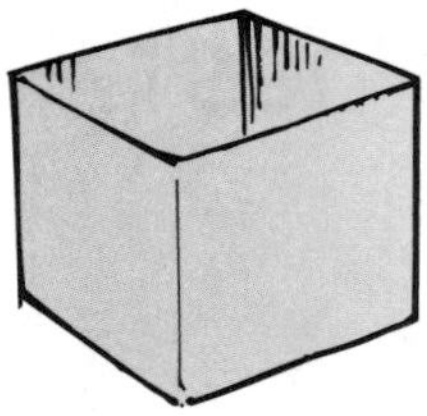

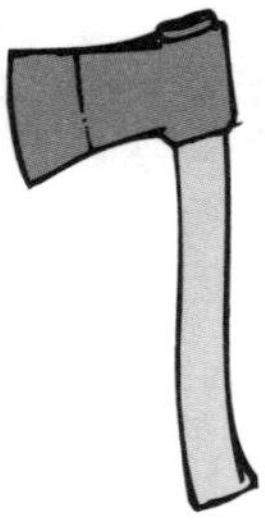

MATH TIME

5 + 2	4 + 4	3 + 3	8 + 0
4 + 2	2 + 5	5 + 3	1 + 7
2 + 6	7 + 1	1 + 6	4 + 3

Draw your house.

List the people who live in your house.

1 2 3 **Count the spaces to find the boxes. Color the boxes to help frog get to the pond.** 4 5 6

over ➡ up ⬆

1. 1 over 4 up
2. 1 over 3 up
3. 2 over 3 up
4. 2 over 2 up
5. 3 over 2 up
6. 4 over 2 up
7. 4 over 1 up

A B C Fill in the missing letters of the alphabet. X Y Z

a ____ c ____ e ____ g

h ____ j ____ l ____ n

o ____ q ____ s ____ u

v ____ x ____ z

Finish the patterns.

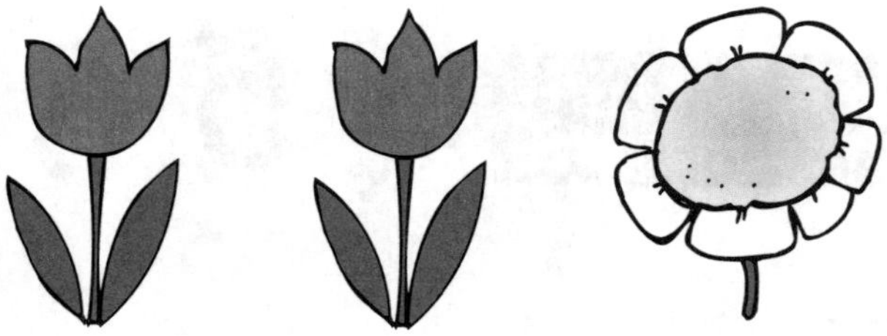 ____ ____ ____

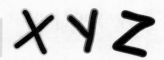

AABB ____ ____ ____ ____

OXX OXX ____ ____ ____

I i

Trace and Write

i i i

I I I

Fill in the missing letters.

p____g

w____g

p____n

____nsects

s____x

f____sh

Color the tallest thing in each box.

Draw the other side of the picture.
Color it the same.

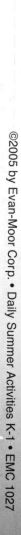

WEEK 9

Color a ★ for each page finished.

		Parent's Initials
Monday	☆ ☆	________
Tuesday	☆ ☆	________
Wednesday	☆ ☆	________
Thursday	☆ ☆	________
Friday	☆ ☆	________

Spelling Words

me

you

What Happened Today? Write about one thing you did each day.

Monday ______________________________

____

____

Tuesday ______________________________

____

____

Wednesday ______________________________

____

____

Thursday ______________________________

____

____

Friday ______________________________

____

____

Keeping Track Color a book for every 10 minutes you read.

Monday Tuesday Wednesday Thursday Friday

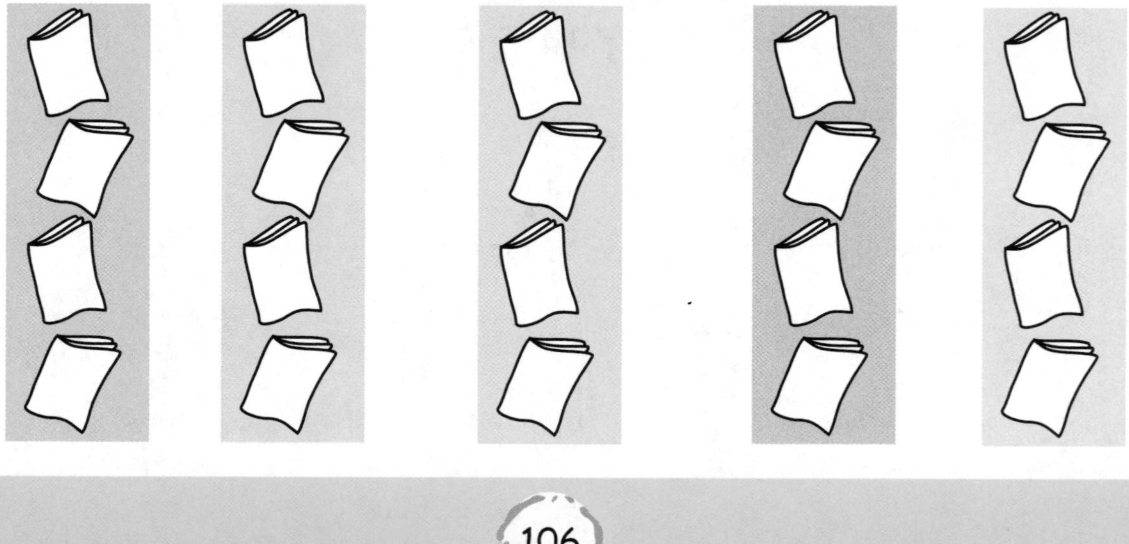

Y y

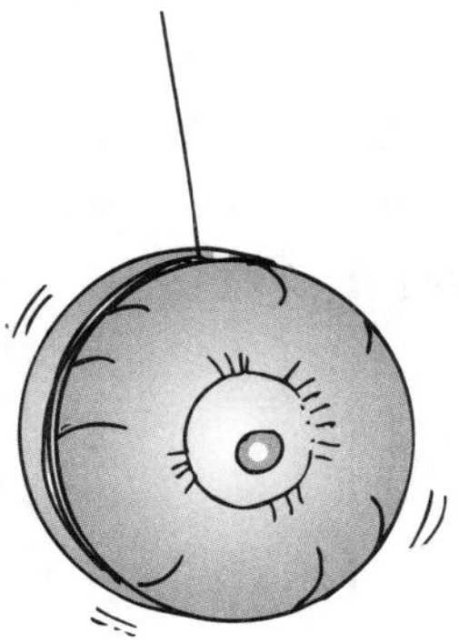

Trace and Write

y y y   Y Y Y

Make an X on the pictures that begin with the sound made by the letter y.

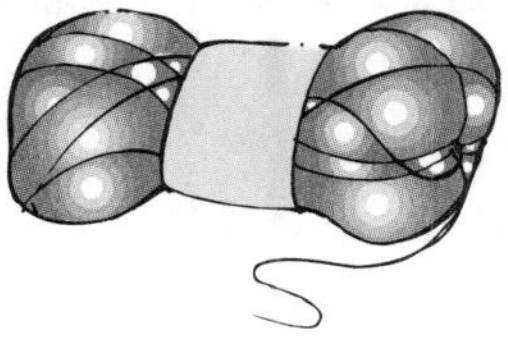

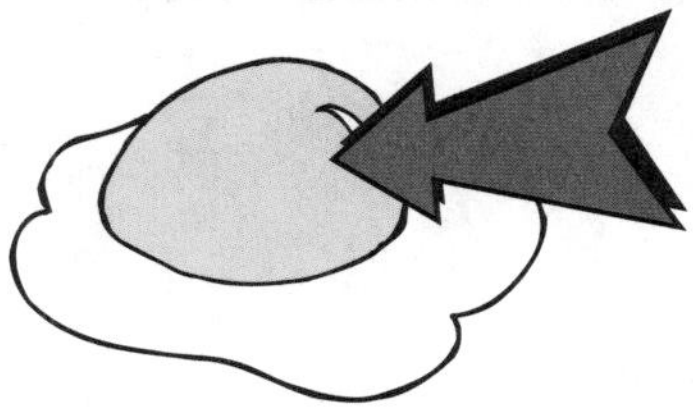

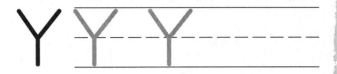

Fill in the missing letters.

a ____oat in a ____oat

a ____ox in a ____ox

Monday

Week 9

Color the pictures that have the sound of i in pig.

Read these words to an adult.

it	sit	fit	hit	bit	mitt
in	bin	fin	pin	tin	win

Trace the numbers to count by 5s.

5¢ 10¢ 15¢ 20¢ 25¢

30¢ 35¢ 40¢ 45¢ 50¢

10  = ______¢

Count to 100 for an adult. **I can count to 100.** yes no

Week 9 Monday

Spell It!

Practice spelling me and you.

Write a letter in each box.

me you

Trace and write the words.

me

you

Copy the sentences using your best handwriting.

Pet the cat.

Sit on the log.

Run and jump.

Write the Words

c a n ___ ___ ___

___ ___ ___

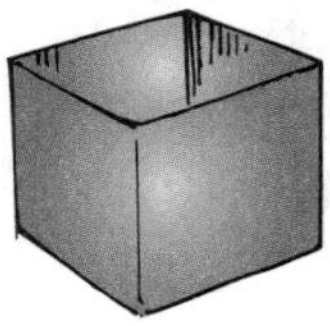

___ ___ ___

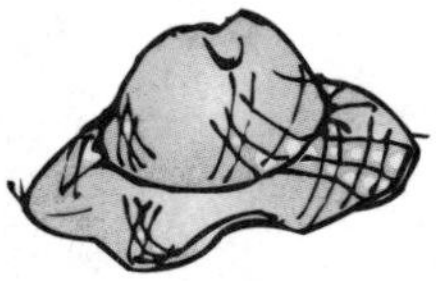

___ ___ ___

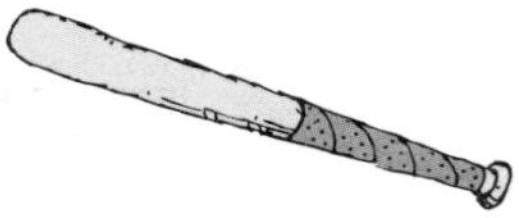

___ ___ ___

___ ___ ___

___ ___ ___

___ ___ ___

___ ___ ___

How many cookies are in the cookie jar?

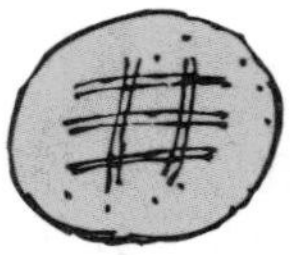 _____

 _____

 _____

How many cookies in all? _____ cookies

Play Ball

glove	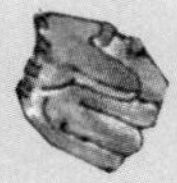
ball	

Tim hit the ball.

Jill ran to get the ball.

Run, Jill, run.

Jill got the ball with her glove.

Number the pictures in order.

Write the names.

Zz

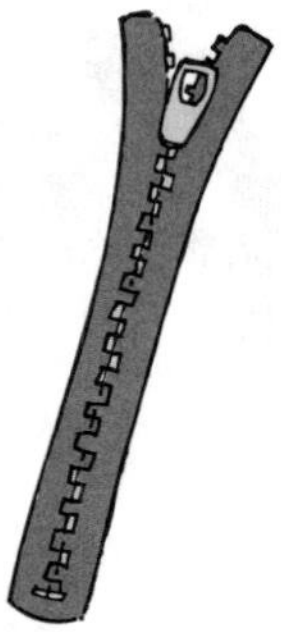

Trace and Write

z z z

Z Z Z

Circle the pictures that begin with the sound made by the letter **z**.

O

Make an **X** on the **heavier** object in each box.

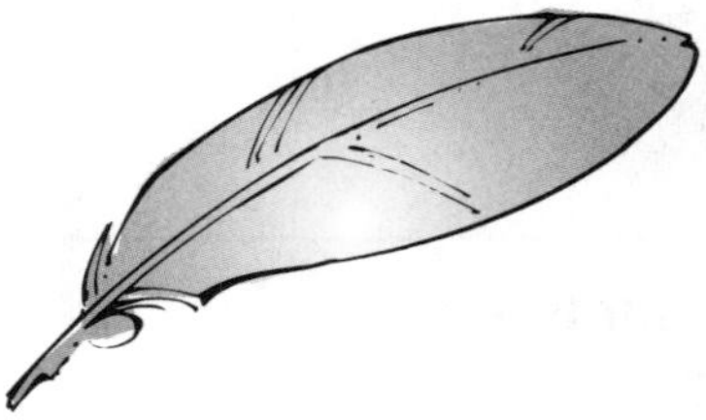

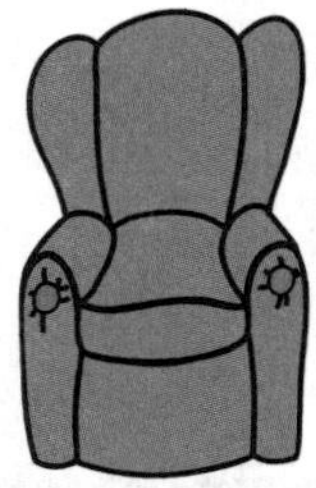

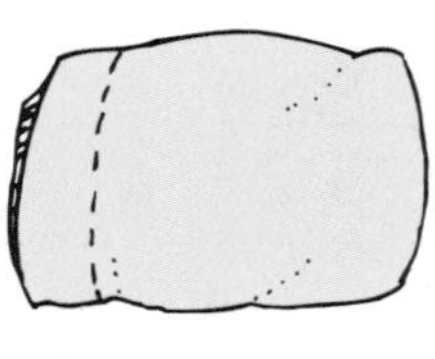

Week 9 Wednesday

Draw an elephant.
Color it.

An elephant ______________________ .

Which way is it?

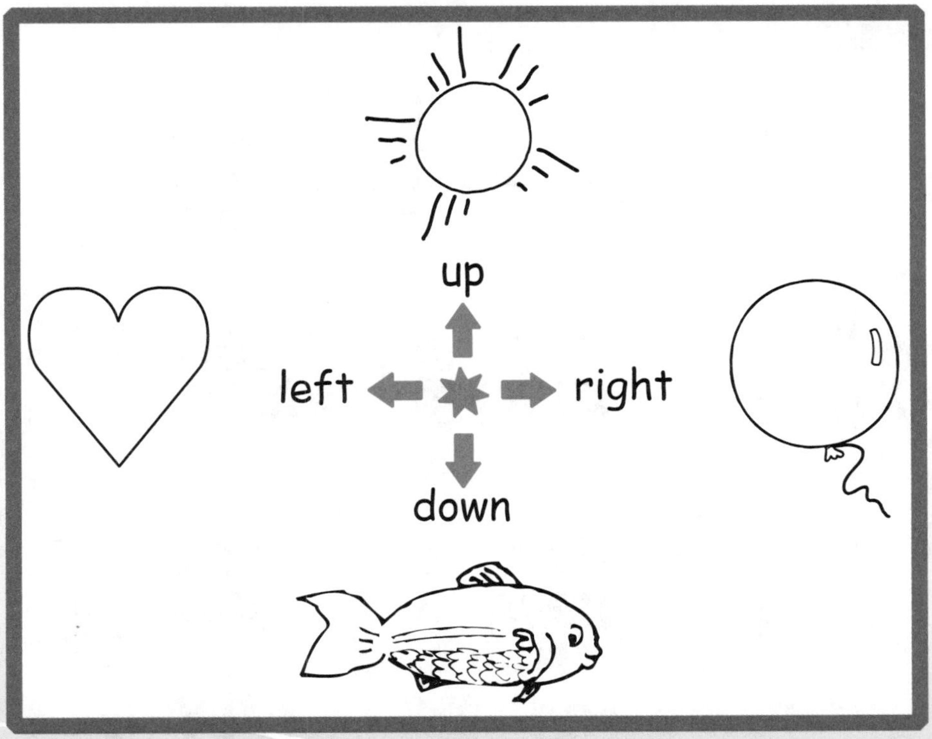

What is **left**?
Color it red.

What is **right**?
Color it blue.

What is **up**?
Color it yellow.

What is **down**?
Color it purple.

Number the pictures in order.

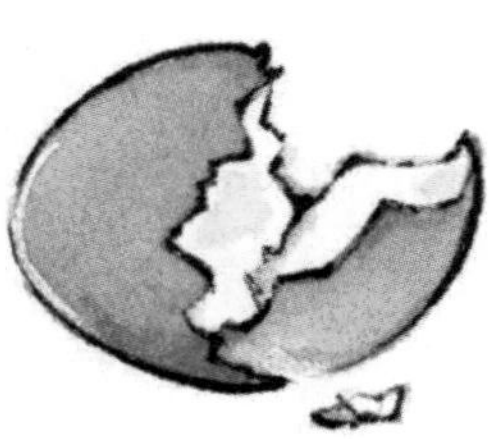

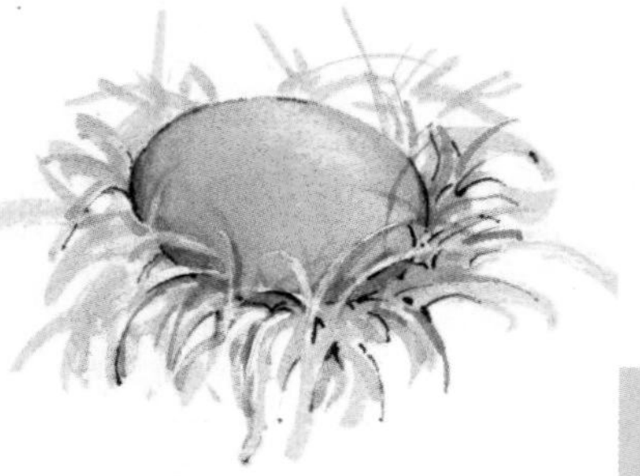

MATH TIME

8 − 2	6 − 1	8 − 4	7 − 3
5 − 2	7 − 4	8 − 5	8 − 8
6 − 3	3 − 1	8 − 3	7 − 5

Oo

Trace and Write

o o o

O O O

Fill in the missing letters.

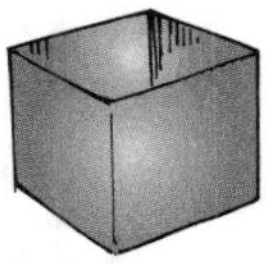

b____x

d____g

f____x

____tter

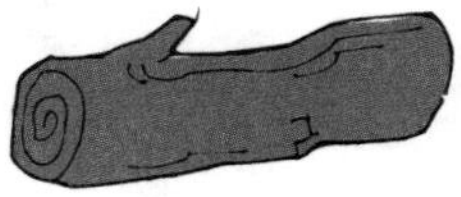

l____g

t____p

ABC Touch each number and read it to an adult. XYZ

9	7	23	6	4	27	15	2	1	17
5	13	22	18	28	30	24	11	16	21
25	3	19	12	20	10	26	8	14	29

I can read the numbers to 30. yes no

Help the cat get the butterfly.
Start at the 1. Color only the number boxes to get to the butterfly.

1	2	3	4	A	B
C	D	E	5	F	G
9	8	7	6	H	I
10	J	K	L	M	N
11	Z	P	16	17	18
12	13	14	15	Q	19

WEEK 10

Color a ☆ for each page finished.

		Parent's Initials
Monday	☆ ☆	________
Tuesday	☆ ☆	________
Wednesday	☆ ☆	________
Thursday	☆ ☆	________
Friday	☆ ☆	________

Spelling Words

and

the

What Happened Today? Write about one thing you did each day.

Monday ______________________________

____

____

Tuesday ______________________________

____

____

Wednesday ______________________________

____

____

Thursday ______________________________

____

____

Friday ______________________________

____

____

Keeping Track Color a book for every 10 minutes you read.

Monday	Tuesday	Wednesday	Thursday	Friday

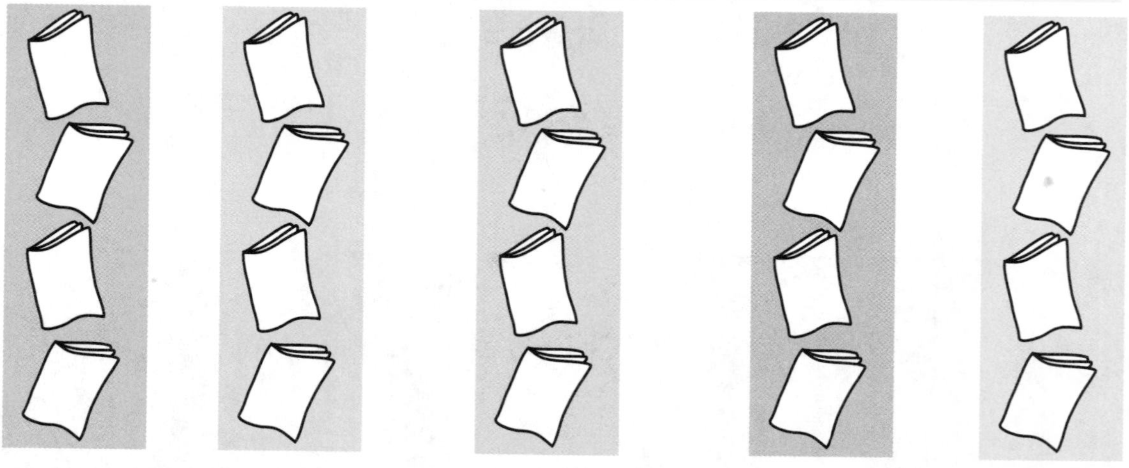

The Pond

A big log is in the pond.

A green frog is on the log.

Jump, frog, jump.

Fill in the missing word.

1. A ______________________ is in the pond.

2. A ______________________ is on the log.

Draw a big brown log.	Draw a green frog.

Uu

Trace and Write

u u u

U U U

Fill in the missing letters.

s____n

b____g

b____s

p____p

n____ts

c____p

Make an **X** on the **smaller** insect in each box.
Circle the **bigger** insect in each box.

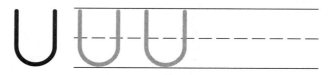

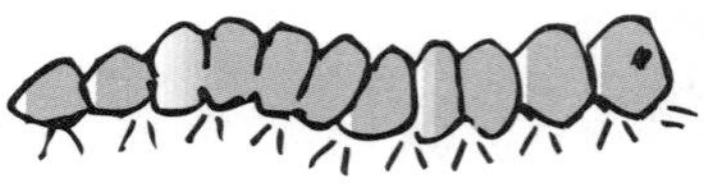

Spell It!

Practice spelling and and the.

Write a letter in each box.

and the

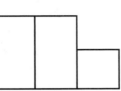

Trace and write the words.

and

the

Copy the sentences using your best handwriting.

A toy fox is in that box.

Six zebras are in the zoo.

Make an X on the pictures in each box that have the same vowel sound.

Trace the Numbers

Count by 10s to an adult. I can count by 10s to 100. yes no

KIM

girl 

bath 

mud 

Kim is a small girl.

She dug in the mud.

She is a mess.

Kim must take a bath.

Match the word to its picture.

Kim 

mud 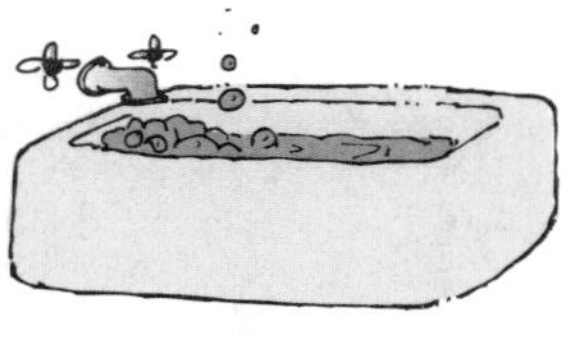

bath 

Color the pictures with the sound of u in cup.

How much money is in each purse?

_________¢

_________¢

_________¢

_________¢

Draw a picture of your family.

My family likes to

____

____.

This is a globe.
It shows Earth.
It shows the land and water.

Color the globe.

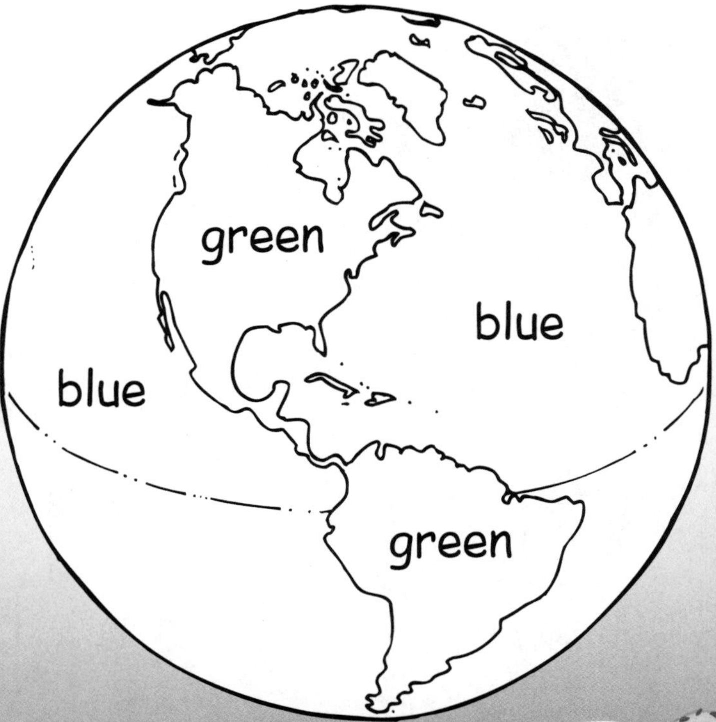

123 456

Circle all of the letters.
Make an X on all of the numbers.

A	9	q	3	N	6
2	P	m	12	Z	8
4	r	t	20	W	L
26	b	5	D	13	10

COLOR THE SHAPES.

red

blue

green

yellow

Write the word to name the picture.

6 s i x

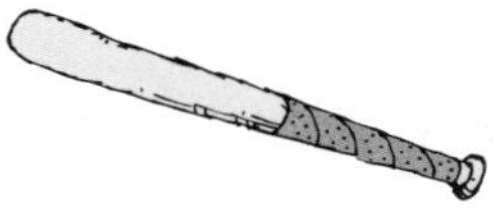 ___ ___ ___

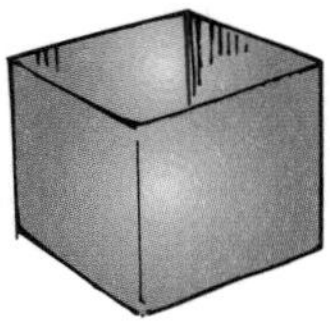 ___ ___ ___

 ___ ___ ___

___ ___ ___

 ___ ___ ___

 ___ ___ ___

 ___ ___ ___

10 ___ ___ ___

 ___ ___ ___

MATH TIME

Use counters if you need help.

6 + 3	2 + 7	4 + 4	9 − 6	5 + 4
9 − 7	3 + 6	9 − 8	9 + 0	1 + 7
7 + 2	9 − 3	0 + 9	8 − 6	9 − 5

Connect the dots from 1 to 30.
Draw someone peeking out of the window.

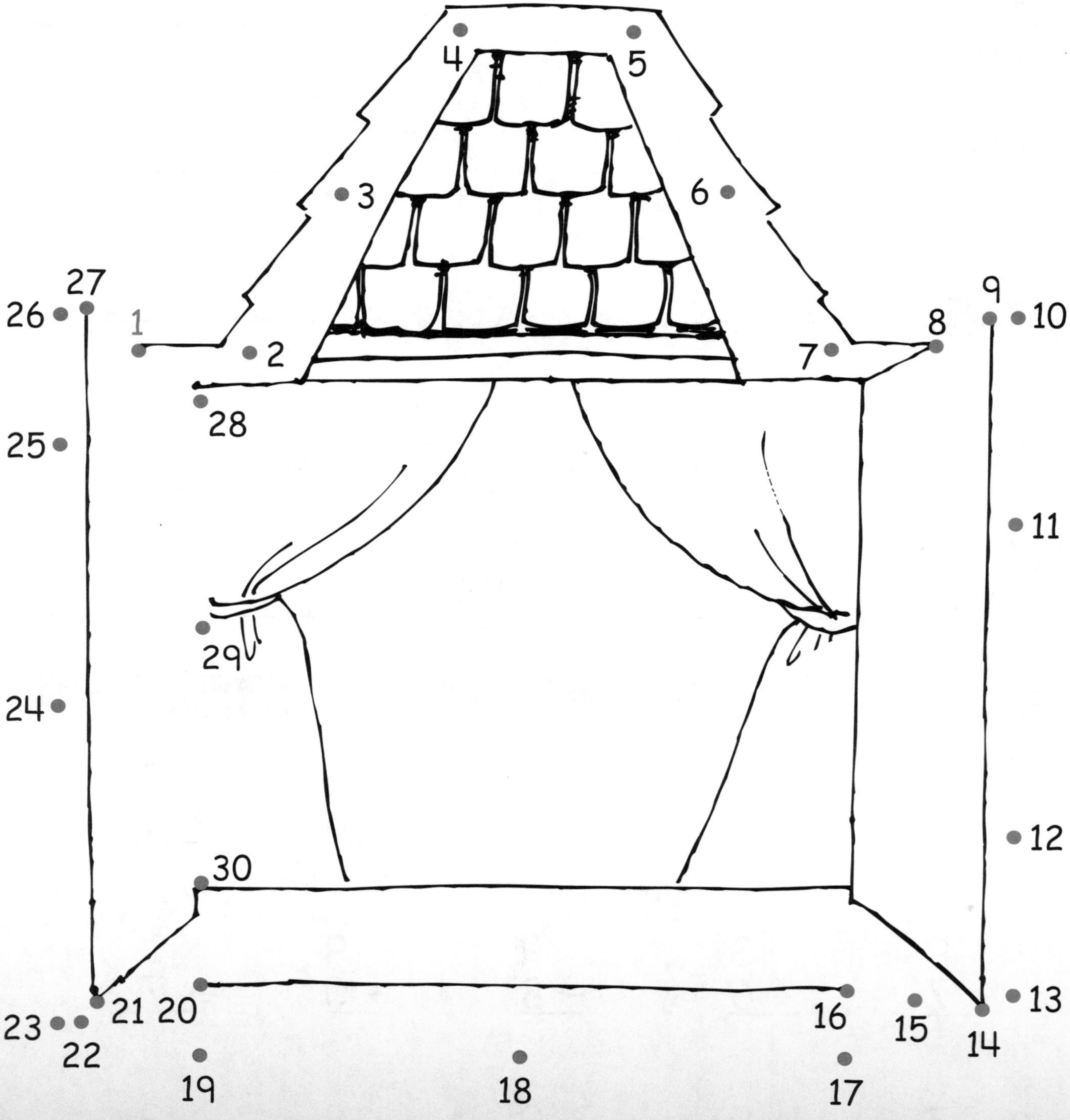

Hooray for Me!

I finished my
summer practice book.
Now, I'm ready for 1st grade!

name

date

Answer Key

Checking your child's work is an important part of learning. It allows you to see what your child knows well and what areas need more practice. It also provides an opportunity for you to help your child understand that making mistakes is a part of learning.

When an error is discovered, ask your child to look carefully at the question or problem. Errors often occur through misreading the problem. Your child can quickly correct these errors.

The answer key pages can be used in several ways:

- Remove the answer pages and give the book to your child. Go over the answers with him or her as each day's work is completed.
- Leave the answer pages in the book and give the practice pages to your child one day at a time.
- Leave the answer pages in the book so your child can check his or her own answers as the pages are completed. It is still important that you review the pages with your child if you use this method.

Page 11

Bb
Trace and Write
b b b B B B
Which pictures begin with the sound made by the letter b? Color them red.
Make an X on the pictures that begin with the same sound.
Monday Week 1 11

Page 12

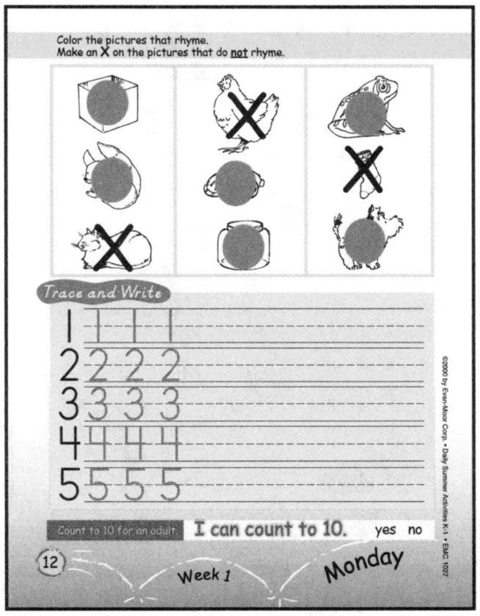

Color the pictures that rhyme.
Make an X on the pictures that do not rhyme.
Trace and Write
1 1 1 1
2 2 2 2
3 3 3 3
4 4 4 4
5 5 5 5
Count to 10 for an adult. I can count to 10. yes no
12 Week 1 Monday

Page 13

Spell It! Practice spelling stop and go.
Write a letter in each box.
go stop
g o s t o p
Trace and write the words.
stop stop stop
go go go
Trace and write the lines.
Tuesday Week 1 13

Page 14

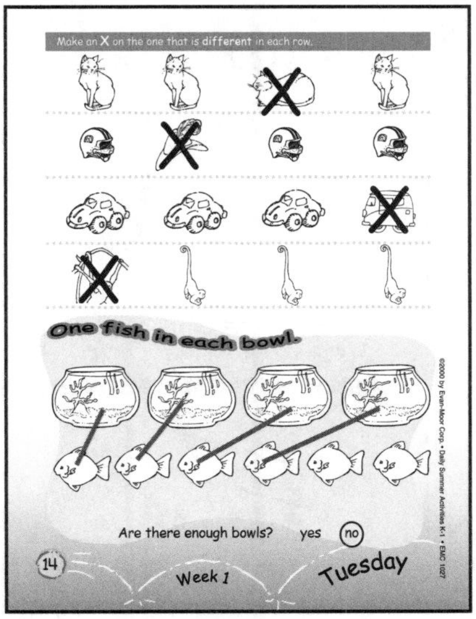

Make an X on the one that is different in each row.
One fish in each bowl.
Are there enough bowls? yes no
14 Week 1 Tuesday

Page 15

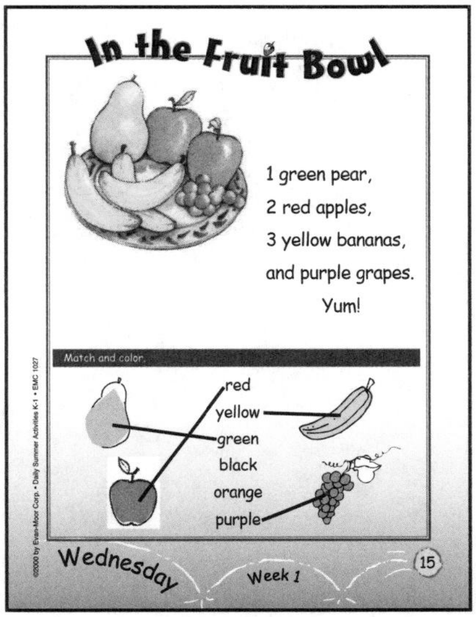

In the Fruit Bowl
1 green pear,
2 red apples,
3 yellow bananas,
and purple grapes.
Yum!
Match and color.
red
yellow
green
black
orange
purple
Wednesday Week 1 15

Page 16

Cc
Trace and Write
c c c C C C
Which pictures begin with the sound made by the letter c? Color them blue.
1 2 3 Color to finish the patterns.
16 Week 1 Wednesday

Page 17

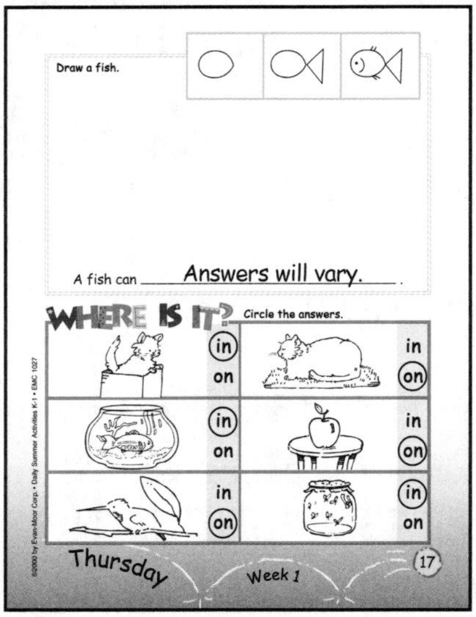
Draw a fish.

A fish can Answers will vary.

WHERE IS IT? Circle the answers.

in on | in on
in on | in on
in on | in on

©2000 by Evan-Moor Corp. • Daily Summer Activities • EMC 1027

Thursday Week 1 17

Page 18

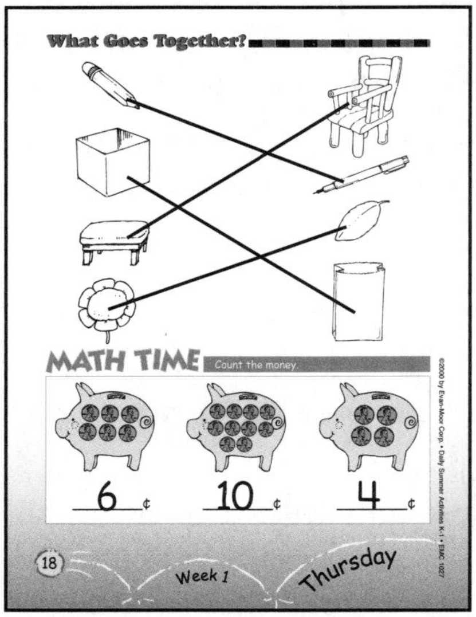
What Goes Together?

MATH TIME Count the money.

6 ¢ 10 ¢ 4 ¢

©2000 by Evan-Moor Corp. • Daily Summer Activities K-1 • EMC 1027

18 Week 1 Thursday

Page 19

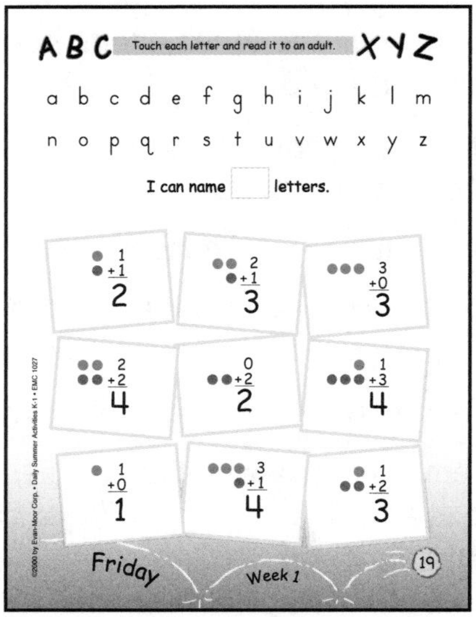
A B C Touch each letter and read it to an adult. X Y Z

a b c d e f g h i j k l m

n o p q r s t u v w x y z

I can name letters.

1 +1 = 2; 2 +1 = 3; 3 +0 = 3

2 +2 = 4; 0 +2 = 2; 1 +3 = 4

1 +0 = 1; 3 +1 = 4; 1 +2 = 3

©2000 by Evan-Moor Corp. • Daily Summer Activities K-1 • EMC 1027

Friday Week 1 19

Page 20

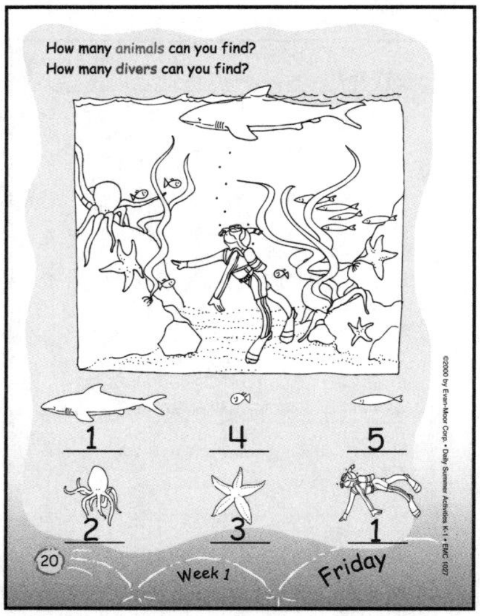
How many animals can you find?

How many divers can you find?

1 4 5

2 3 1

©2000 by Evan-Moor Corp. • Daily Summer Activities K-1 • EMC 1027

20 Week 1 Friday

Page 23

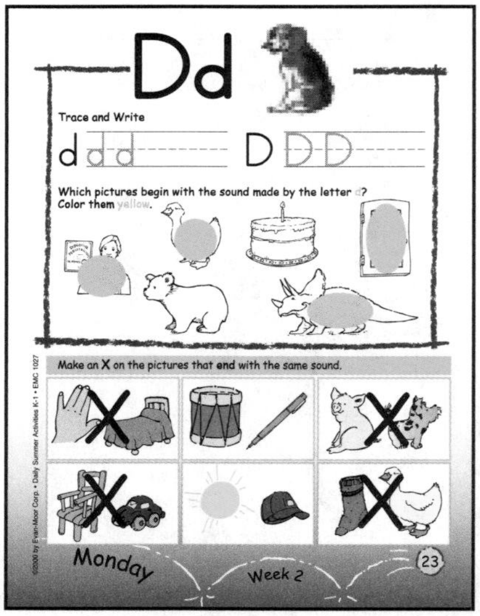
Dd

Trace and Write

d d d D D D

Which pictures begin with the sound made by the letter d?

Color them yellow.

Make an X on the pictures that end with the same sound.

©2000 by Evan-Moor Corp. • Daily Summer Activities K-1 • EMC 1027

Monday Week 2 23

Page 24

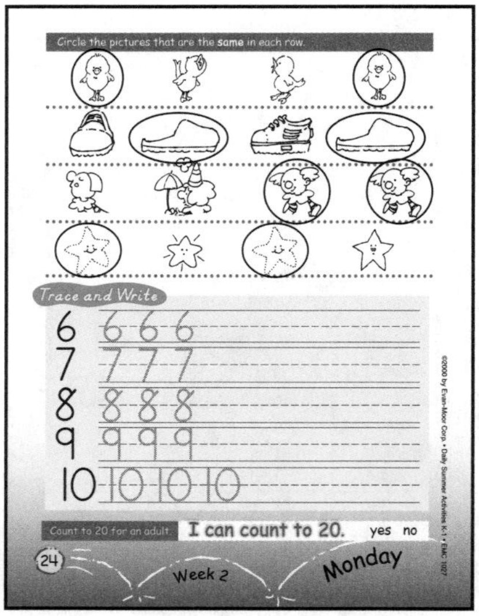
Circle the pictures that are the same in each row.

Trace and Write

6 6 6 6

7 7 7 7

8 8 8 8

9 9 9 9

10 10 10 10

Count to 20 for an adult. I can count to 20. yes no

©2000 by Evan-Moor Corp. • Daily Summer Activities K-1 • EMC 1027

24 Week 2 Monday

Page 25

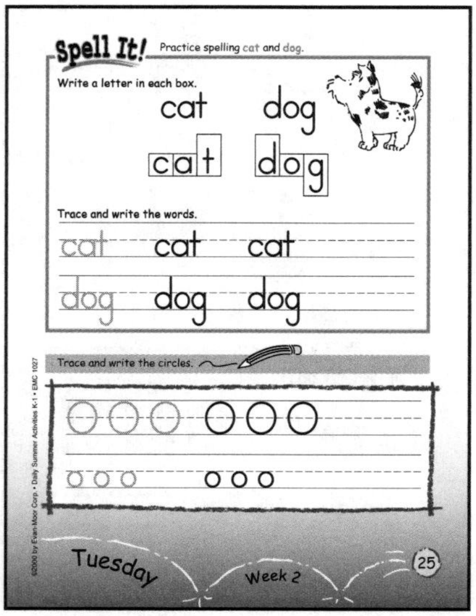
Spell It! Practice spelling cat and dog.

Write a letter in each box.

cat dog

cat dog

Trace and write the words.

cat cat cat

dog dog dog

Trace and write the circles.

O O O O O O

o o o o o o

©2000 by Evan-Moor Corp. • Daily Summer Activities K-1 • EMC 1027

Tuesday Week 2 25

Page 26

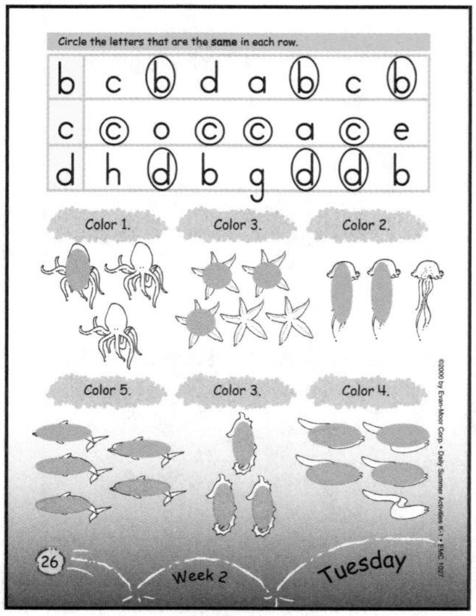
Circle the letters that are the same in each row.

b c b d a b c b

c c o c c a c e

d h d b g d d b

Color 1. Color 3. Color 2.

Color 5. Color 3. Color 4.

©2000 by Evan-Moor Corp. • Daily Summer Activities K-1 • EMC 1027

26 Week 2 Tuesday

Page 27

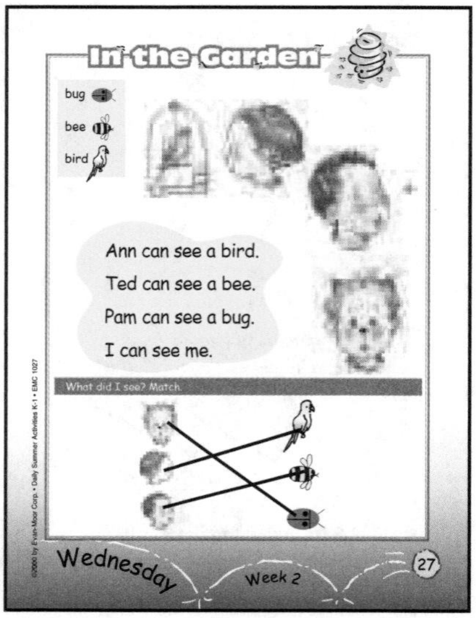
In the Garden

bug

bee

bird

Ann can see a bird.

Ted can see a bee.

Pam can see a bug.

I can see me.

What did I see? Match.

©2000 by Evan-Moor Corp. • Daily Summer Activities K-1 • EMC 1027

Wednesday Week 2 27

Page 28

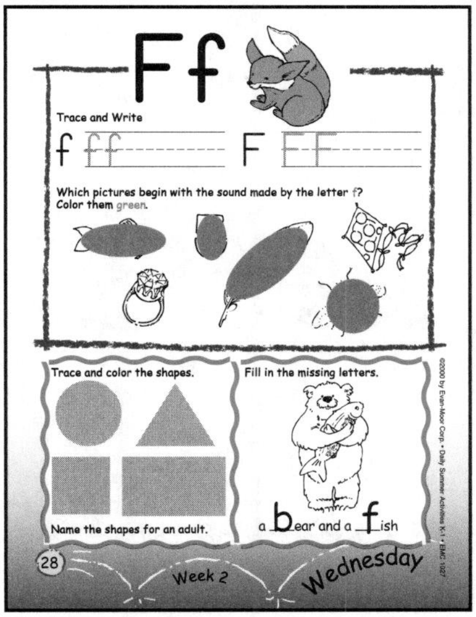
Ff

Trace and Write

Which pictures begin with the sound made by the letter f? Color them green.

Trace and color the shapes.

Name the shapes for an adult.

Fill in the missing letters.

a b ear and a f ish

28 Week 2 Wednesday

Page 29

Copy the picture and color it the same.

My sailboat can Answers will vary.

WHERE IS IT? Circle the answers.

up down in out

up down up down

in out in out

Thursday Week 2 29

Page 30

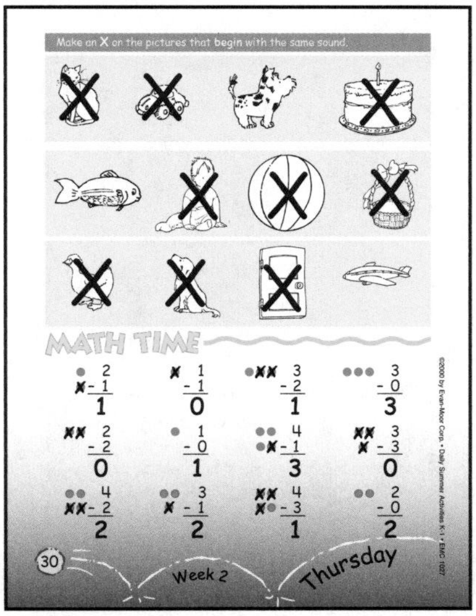
Make an X on the pictures that begin with the same sound.

MATH TIME

2 − 1 = 1; 1 − 1 = 0; 3 − 2 = 1; 3 − 0 = 3

2 − 2 = 0; 1 − 0 = 1; 4 − 1 = 3; 3 − 3 = 0

4 − 2 = 2; 3 − 1 = 2; 4 − 3 = 1; 2 − 0 = 2

30 Week 2 Thursday

Page 31

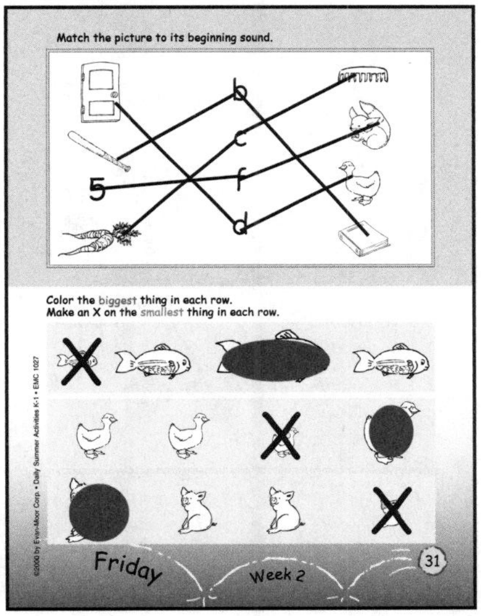
Match the picture to its beginning sound.

b c f d

Color the biggest thing in each row. Make an X on the smallest thing in each row.

Friday Week 2 31

Page 32

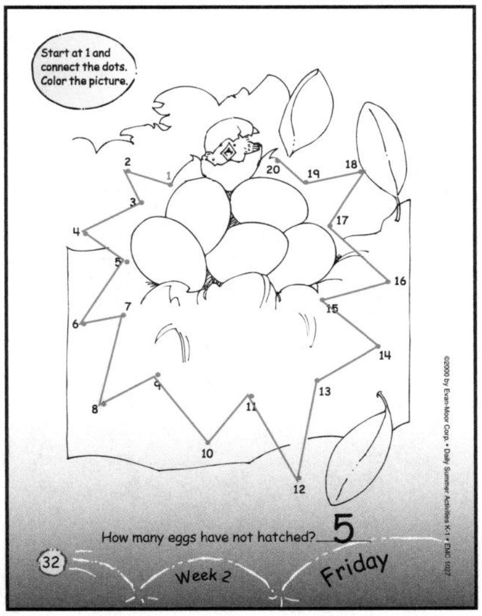
Start at 1 and connect the dots. Color the picture.

How many eggs have not hatched? 5

32 Week 2 Friday

Page 35

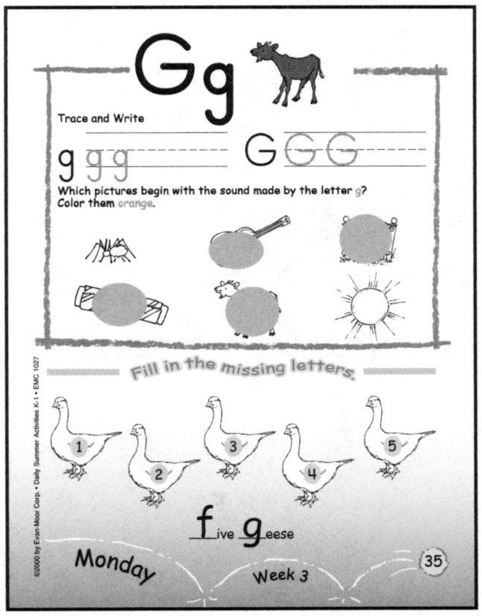
Gg

Trace and Write

Which pictures begin with the sound made by the letter g? Color them orange.

Fill in the missing letters.

f ive g eese

Monday Week 3 35

Page 36

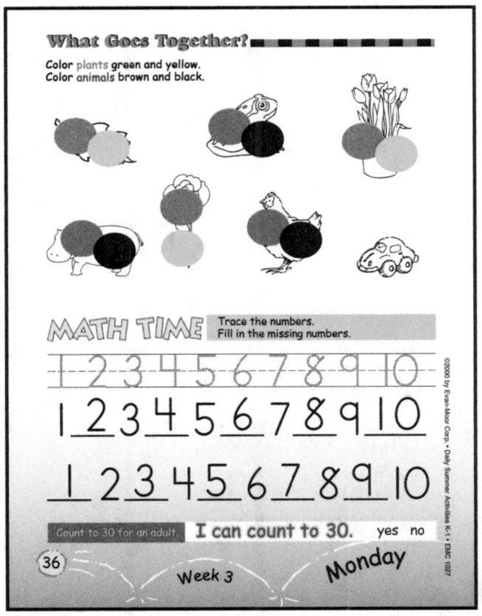
What Goes Together?

Color plants green and yellow. Color animals brown and black.

MATH TIME Trace the numbers. Fill in the missing numbers.

1 2 3 4 5 6 7 8 9 10

1 2 3 4 5 6 7 8 9 10

1 2 3 4 5 6 7 8 9 10

Count to 30 for an adult. I can count to 30. yes no

36 Week 3 Monday

Page 37

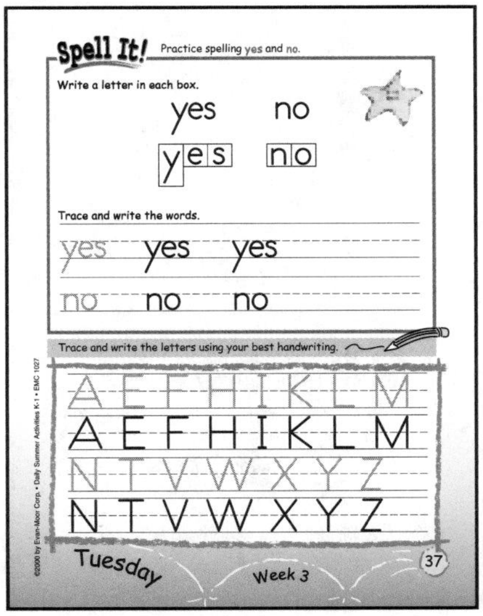
Spell It! Practice spelling yes and no.

Write a letter in each box.

yes no

yes no

Trace and write the words.

yes yes yes

no no no

Trace and write the letters using your best handwriting.

A E F H I K L M

A E F H I K L M

N T V W X Y Z

N T V W X Y Z

Tuesday Week 3 37

Page 38

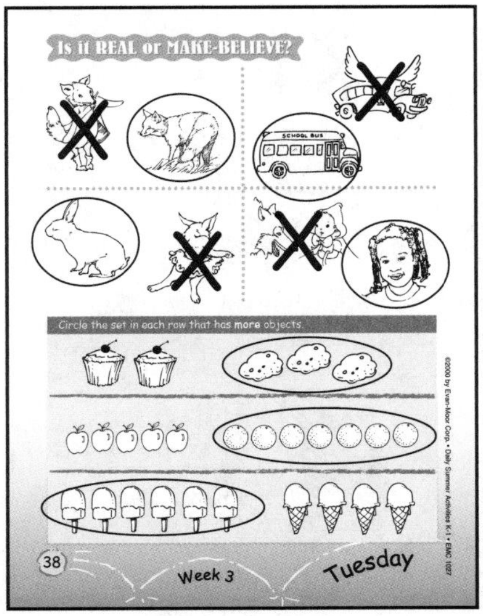
Is it REAL or MAKE-BELIEVE?

Circle the set in each row that has more objects.

38 Week 3 Tuesday

Page 39

CATS
Cats can run.
Cats can hop.
Cats can jump.
Cats can stop.
Circle the words that rhyme.
1. hop wash shop
2. stop mop jump
3. top run pop
Wednesday
Week 3
39

Page 40

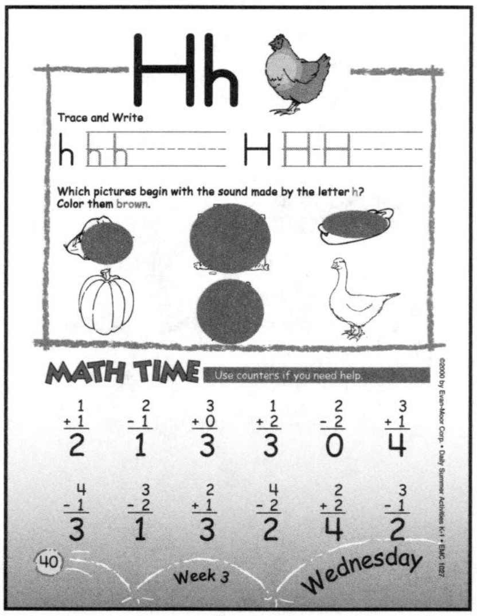
Hh
Trace and Write
Which pictures begin with the sound made by the letter h?
Color them brown.
MATH TIME
Use counters if you need help.
1 +1 = 2
2 -1 = 1
3 +0 = 3
1 +2 = 3
2 -2 = 0
3 +1 = 4
4 -1 = 3
3 -2 = 1
2 +1 = 3
4 -2 = 2
2 +2 = 4
3 -1 = 2
40
Week 3
Wednesday

Page 41

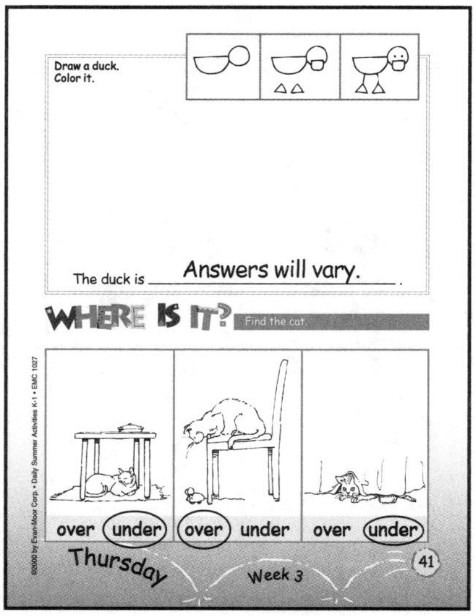
Draw a duck.
Color it.
The duck is Answers will vary.
WHERE IS IT?
Find the cat.
over under
over under
over under
Thursday
Week 3
41

Page 42

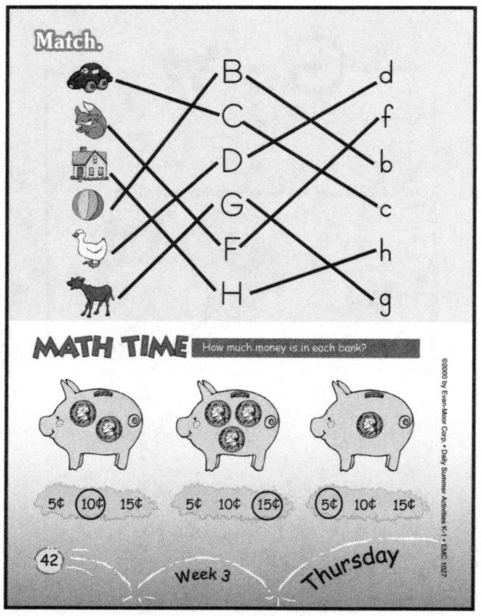
Match.
B
C
D
G
F
H
d
f
b
c
h
g
MATH TIME
How much money is in each bank?
5¢ 10¢ 15¢
5¢ 10¢ 15¢
5¢ 10¢ 15¢
42
Week 3
Thursday

Page 43

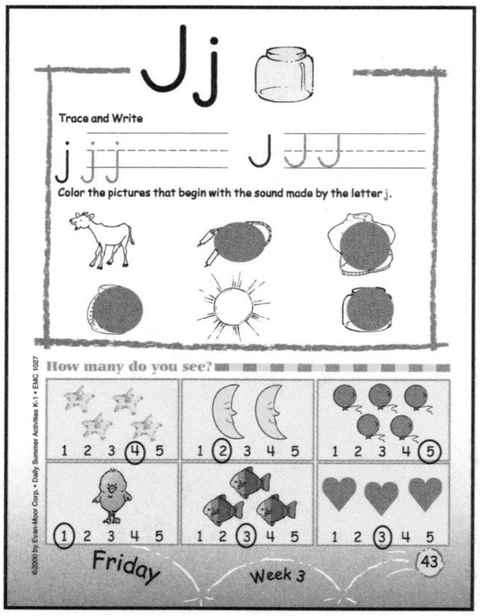
Jj
Trace and Write
Color the pictures that begin with the sound made by the letter j.
How many do you see?
1 2 3 4 5
Friday
Week 3
43

Page 44

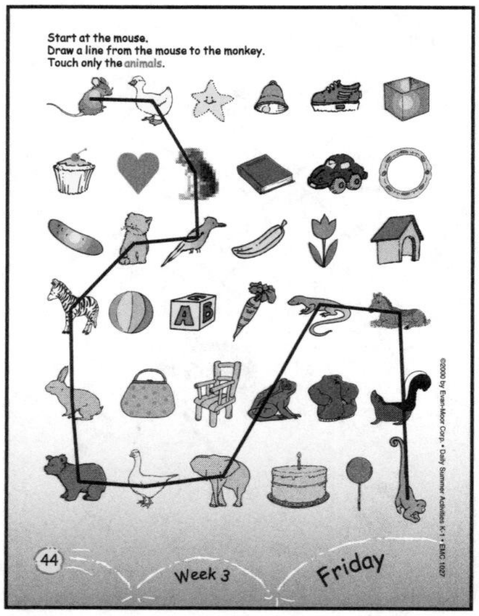
Start at the mouse.
Draw a line from the mouse to the monkey.
Touch only the animals.
44
Week 3
Friday

Page 47

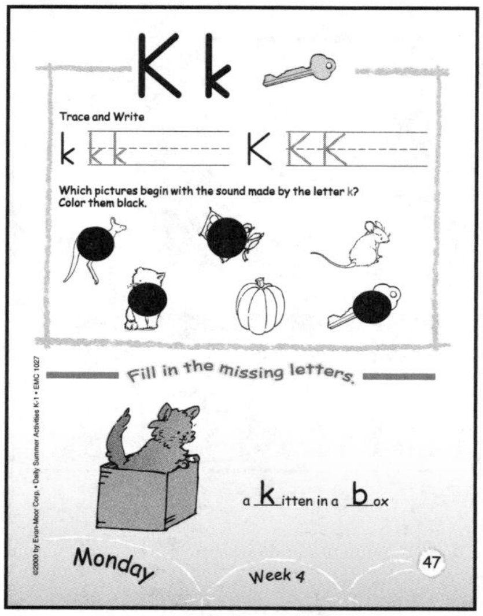
Kk
Trace and Write
Which pictures begin with the sound made by the letter k?
Color them black.
Fill in the missing letters.
a kitten in a box
Monday
Week 4
47

Page 48

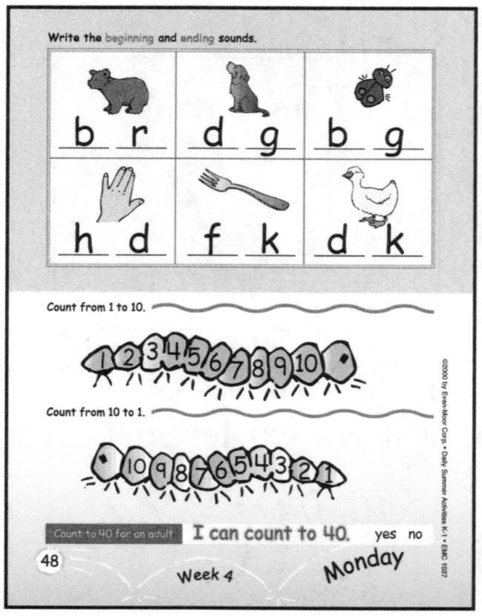
Write the beginning and ending sounds.
b r
d g
b g
h d
f k
d k
Count from 1 to 10.
1 2 3 4 5 6 7 8 9 10
Count from 10 to 1.
10 9 8 7 6 5 4 3 2 1
Count to 40 for an adult.
I can count to 40. yes no
48
Week 4
Monday

Page 49

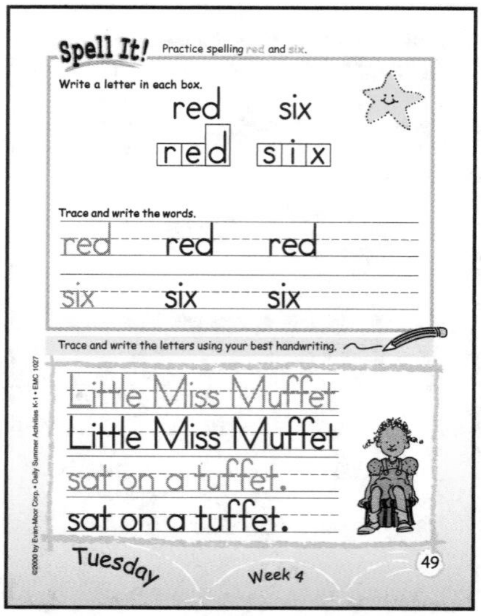
Spell It! Practice spelling red and six.
Write a letter in each box.
red six
red six
Trace and write the words.
red red red
six six six
Trace and write the letters using your best handwriting.
Little Miss Muffet
Little Miss Muffet
sat on a tuffet.
sat on a tuffet.
Tuesday
Week 4
49

Page 50

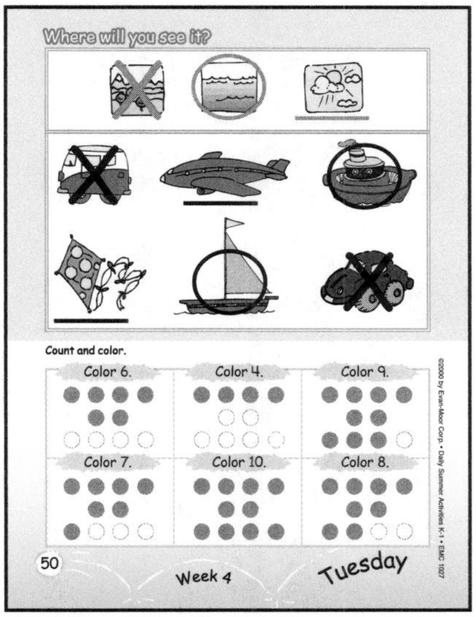
Where will you see it?

Count and color.

Color 6. Color 4. Color 9.

Color 7. Color 10. Color 8.

50 Week 4 Tuesday

Page 51

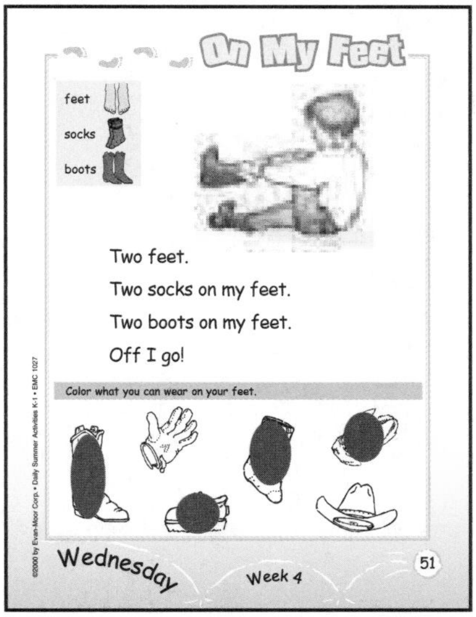
On My Feet

feet

socks

boots

Two feet.

Two socks on my feet.

Two boots on my feet.

Off I go!

Color what you can wear on your feet.

Wednesday Week 4 51

Page 52

L l

Trace and Write

Circle the pictures that begin with the sound made by the letter l.

Trace the numbers on the clock.

Color the big hand green.

Color the little hand blue.

52 Week 4 Wednesday

Page 53

Draw a wagon.

I carry Answers will vary. in my wagon.

Make an X on the left hand. Color the right hand.

Make an X on the right boot. Color the left boot.

Thursday Week 4 53

Page 54

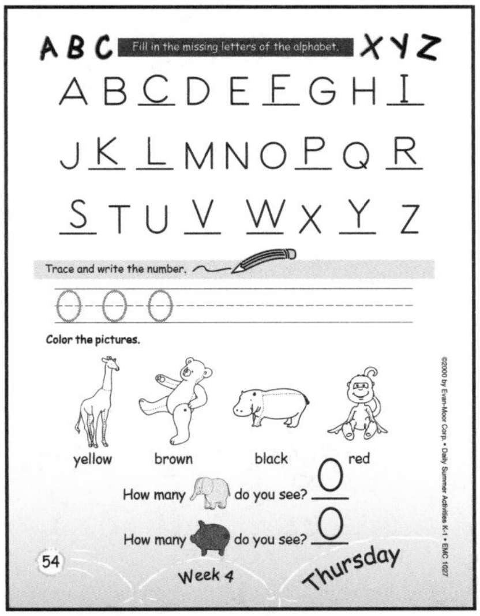
A B C Fill in the missing letters of the alphabet. X Y Z

A B C D E F G H I

J K L M N O P Q R

S T U V W X Y Z

Trace and write the number.

Color the pictures.

yellow brown black red

How many do you see? 0

How many do you see? 0

54 Week 4 Thursday

Page 55

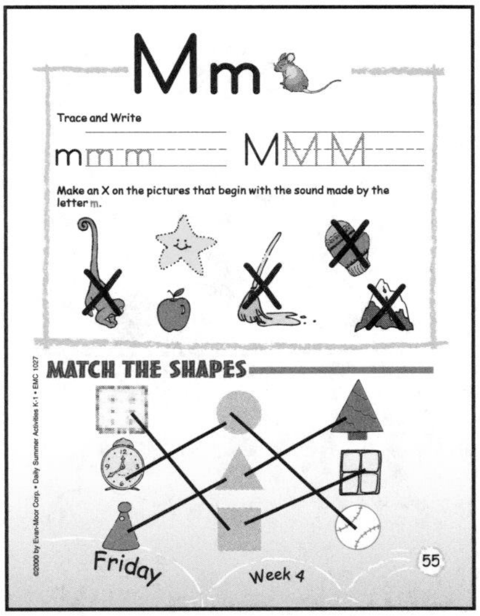
Mm

Trace and Write

Make an X on the pictures that begin with the sound made by the letter m.

MATCH THE SHAPES

Friday Week 4 55

Page 56

Draw the other side. Color it the same.

56 Week 4 Friday

Page 59

Nn

Trace and Write

Circle the pictures that begin with the sound made by the letter n.

Fill in the missing letters.

a dog in a boat

nuts in a box

Monday Week 5 59

Page 60

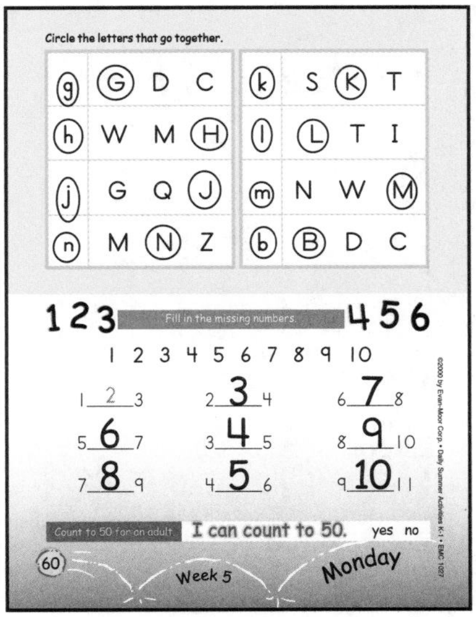
Circle the letters that go together.

g	G	D	C	k	S	K	T
h	W	M	H	l	L	T	I
j	G	Q	J	m	N	W	M
n	M	N	Z	b	B	D	C

1 2 3 Fill in the missing numbers. 4 5 6

1 2 3 4 5 6 7 8 9 10

1 2 3 2 3 4 6 7 8

5 6 7 3 4 5 8 9 10

7 8 9 4 5 6 9 10 11

Count to 50 for an adult. I can count to 50. yes no

60 Week 5 Monday

Page 61

Spell It! Practice spelling run and jump.

Write a letter in each box.

run jump

Trace and write the words.

run run run

jump jump jump

Trace and write the letters using your best handwriting.

Humpty Dumpty

Humpty Dumpty

sat on a wall.

sat on a wall.

Tuesday Week 5 61

Page 62

Match the pictures that are opposites.

Draw dots on the clown hats.

5 9 8 6 10 7

62 Week 5 Tuesday

Page 63

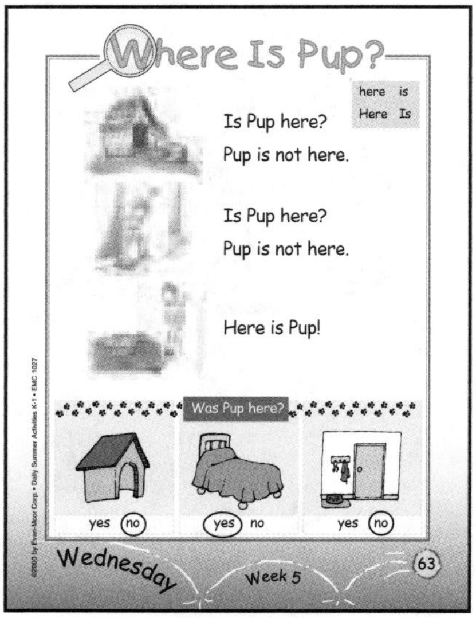
Where Is Pup?

here is Here Is

Is Pup here?

Pup is not here.

Is Pup here?

Pup is not here.

Here is Pup!

Was Pup here?

yes no yes no yes no

Wednesday Week 5 63

Page 64

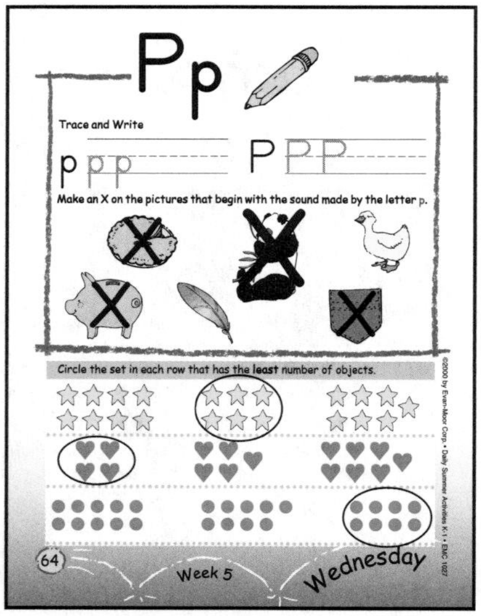
Pp

Trace and Write

p p p P P P

Make an X on the pictures that begin with the sound made by the letter p.

Circle the set in each row that has the least number of objects.

64 Week 5 Wednesday

Page 65

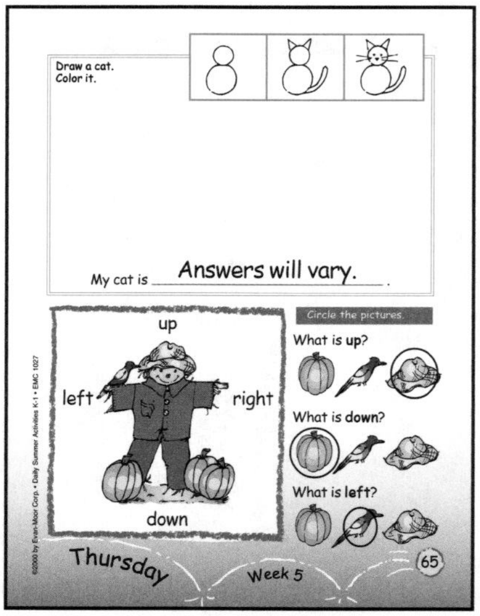
Draw a cat. Color it.

My cat is Answers will vary.

up left right down

Circle the pictures.

What is up?

What is down?

What is left?

Thursday Week 5 65

Page 66

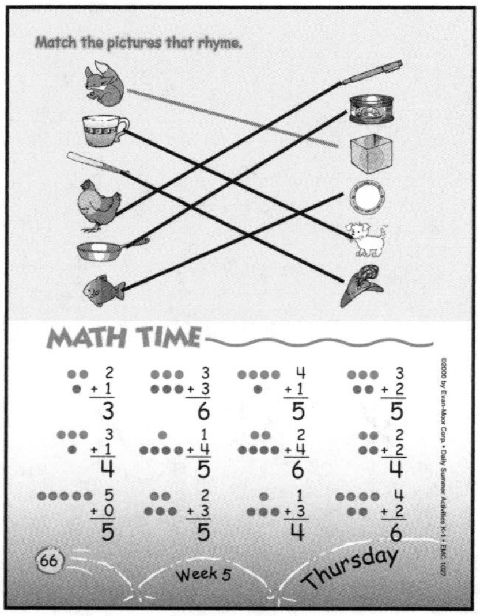
Match the pictures that rhyme.

MATH TIME

2 + 1 = 3	3 + 3 = 6	4 + 1 = 5	3 + 2 = 5
3 + 1 = 4	1 + 4 = 5	2 + 4 = 6	2 + 2 = 4
5 + 0 = 5	2 + 3 = 5	1 + 3 = 4	4 + 2 = 6

66 Week 5 Thursday

Page 67

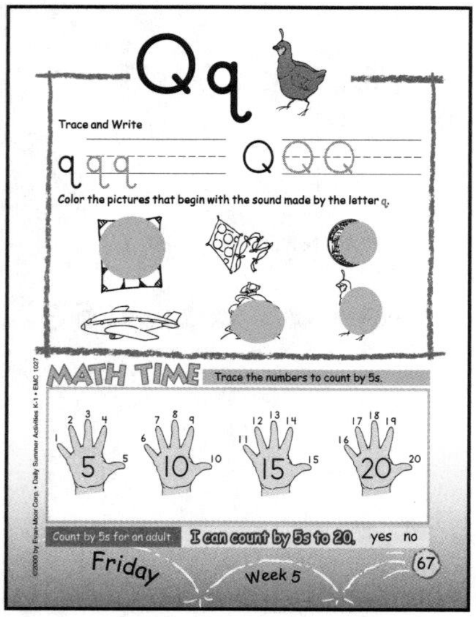
Qq

Trace and Write

q q q Q Q Q

Color the pictures that begin with the sound made by the letter q.

MATH TIME Trace the numbers to count by 5s.

5 10 15 20

Count by 5s for an adult. I can count by 5s to 20. yes no

Friday Week 5 67

Page 68

Start at A and connect the dots. Color the picture.

Rags

68 Week 5 Friday

Page 71

Rr

Trace and Write

r r r R R R

Color the pictures that begin with the sound made by the letter r.

Fill in the missing letters.

the queen had a quilt a robot had a dog

Monday Week 6 71

Page 72

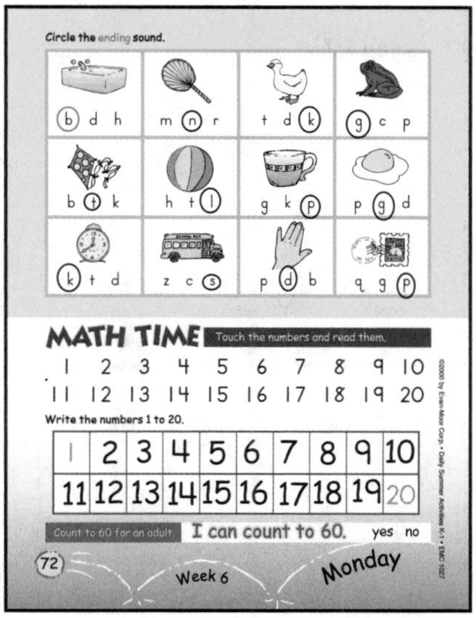

Page 73

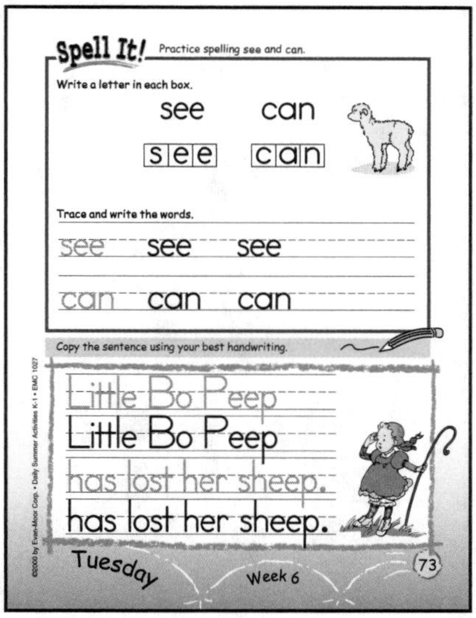

Page 74

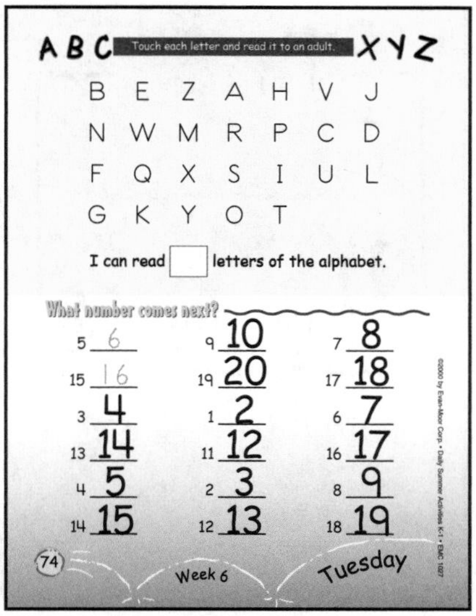

Page 75

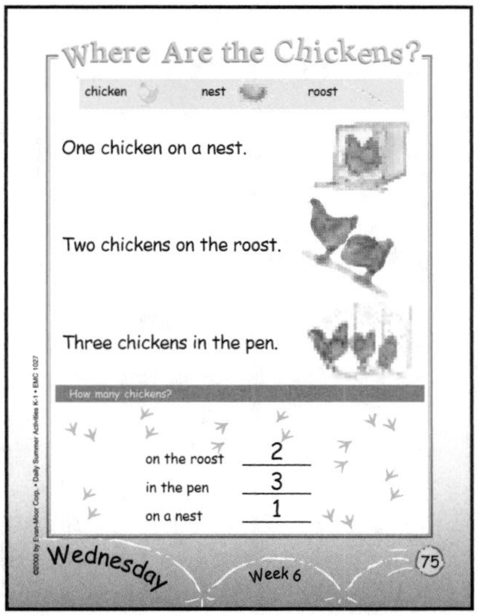

Page 76

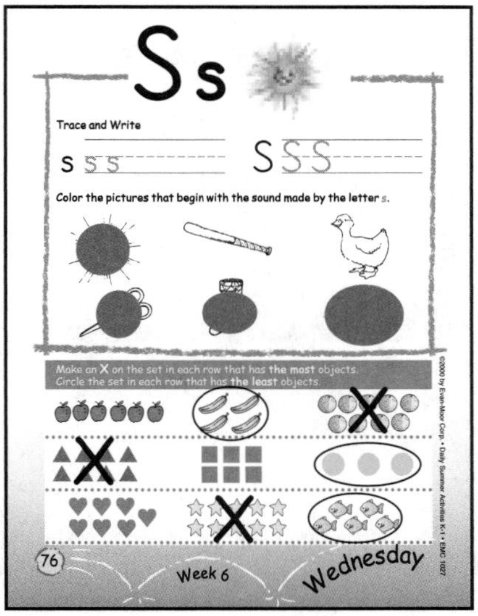

Page 77

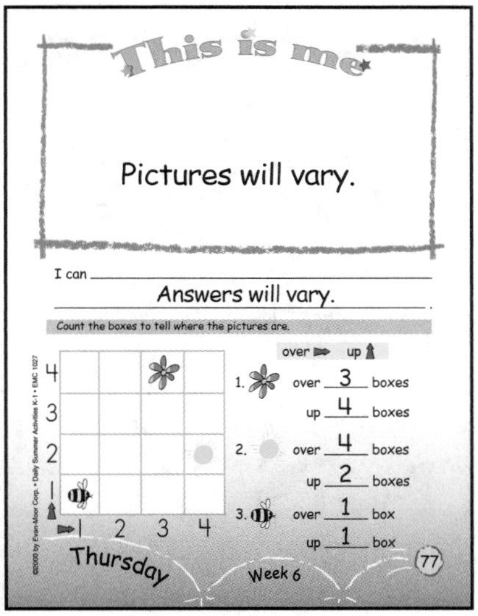

Page 78

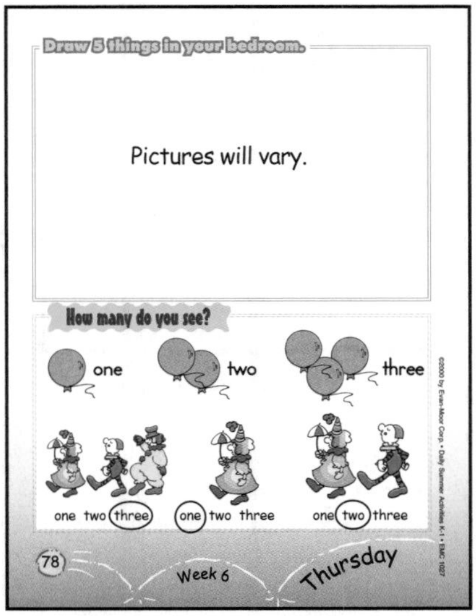

Page 79

Page 80

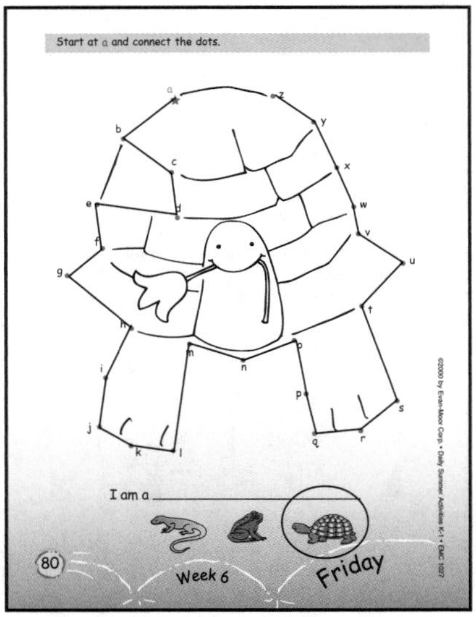

Page 83

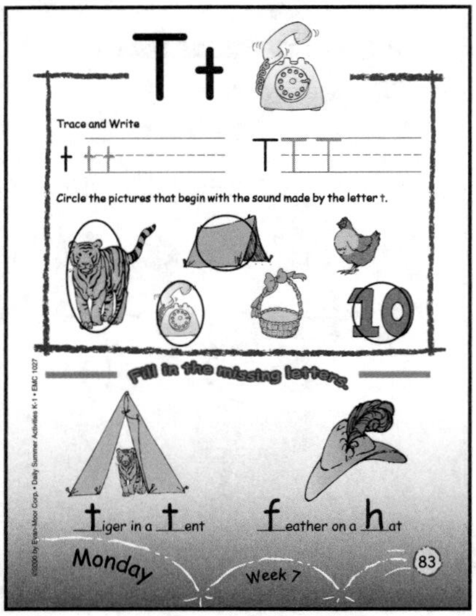

Page 84

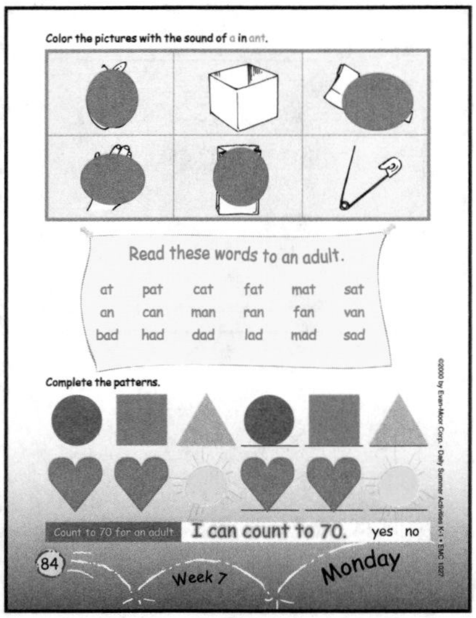

Page 85

Page 86

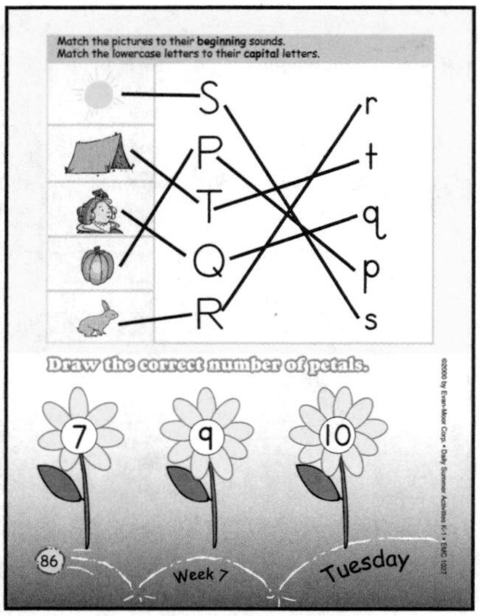

Page 87

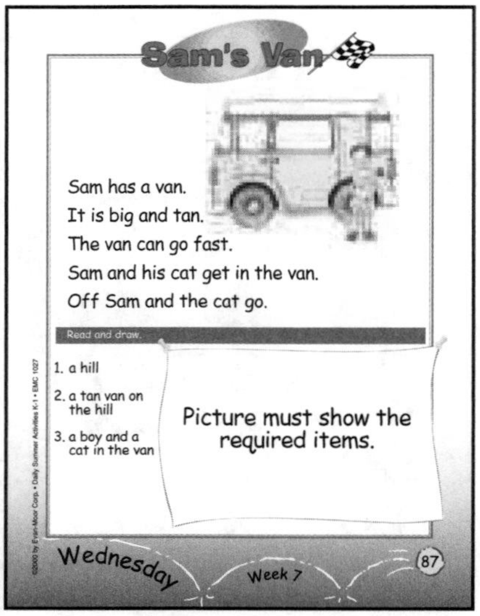

Page 88

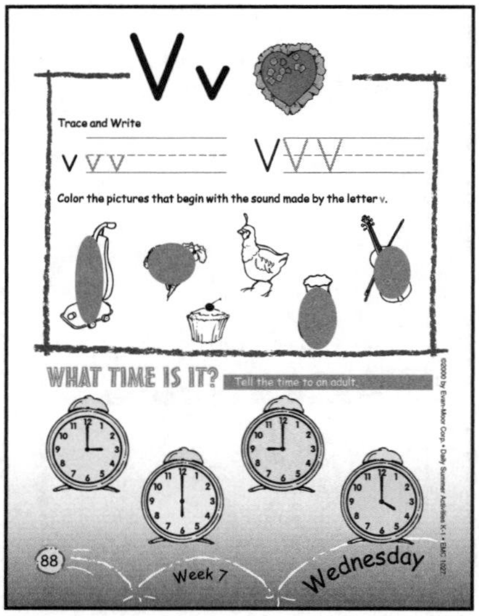

Page 89

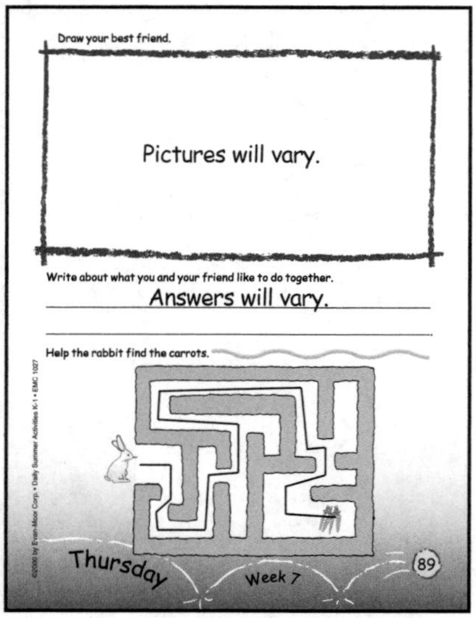

Page 90

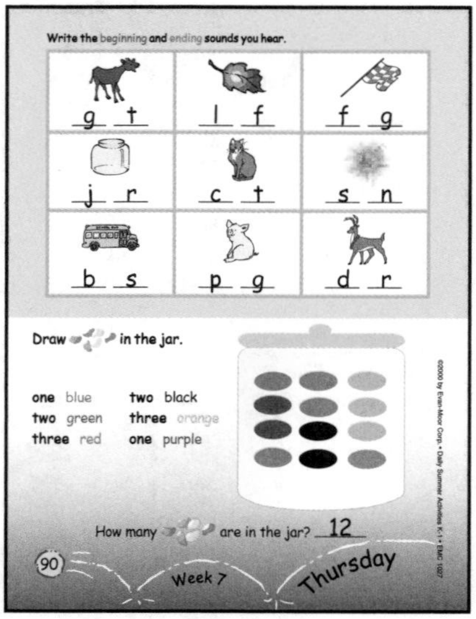

Page 91

Page 92

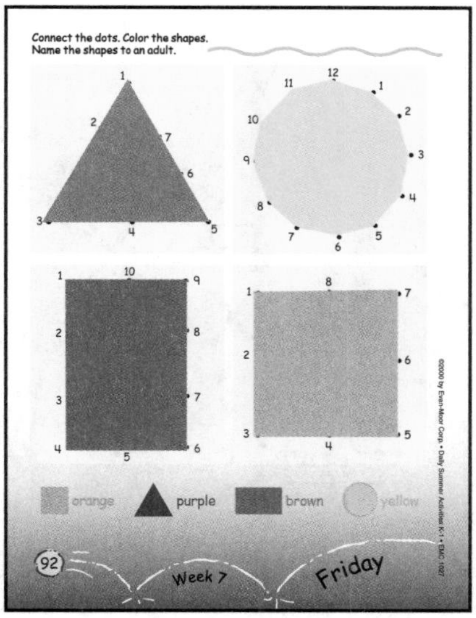

Page 95

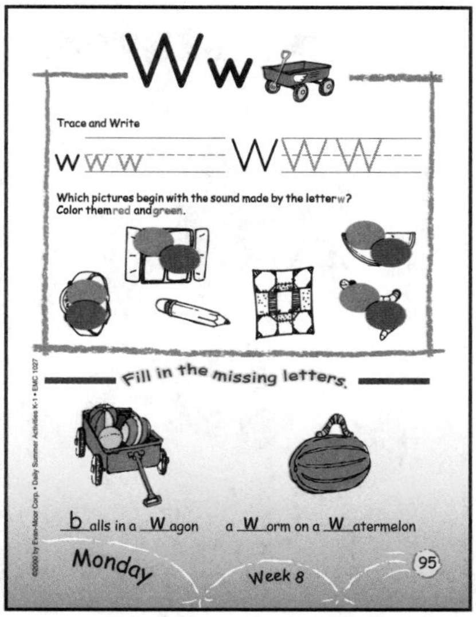

Page 96

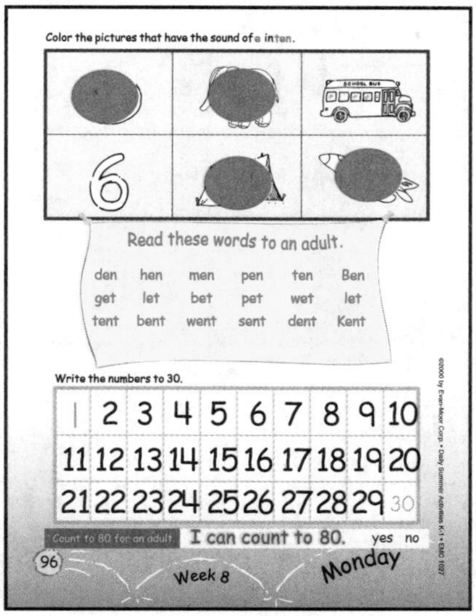

Page 97

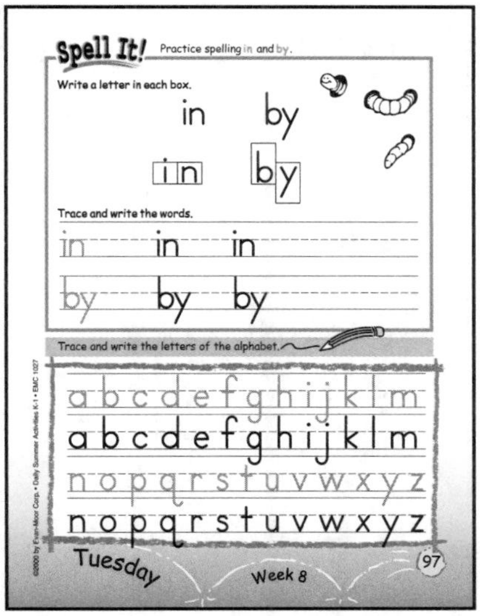

Page 98

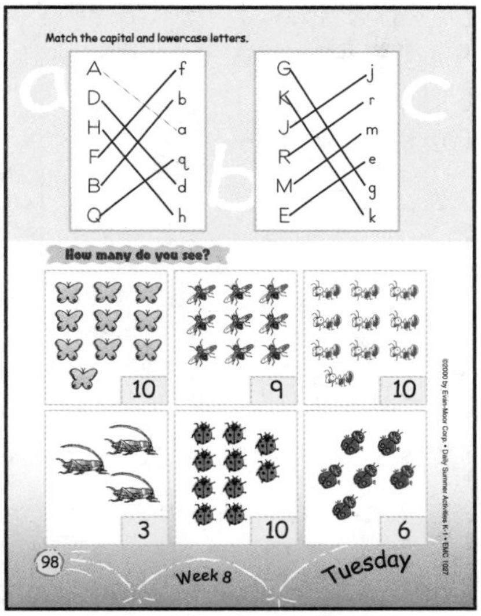

Page 99

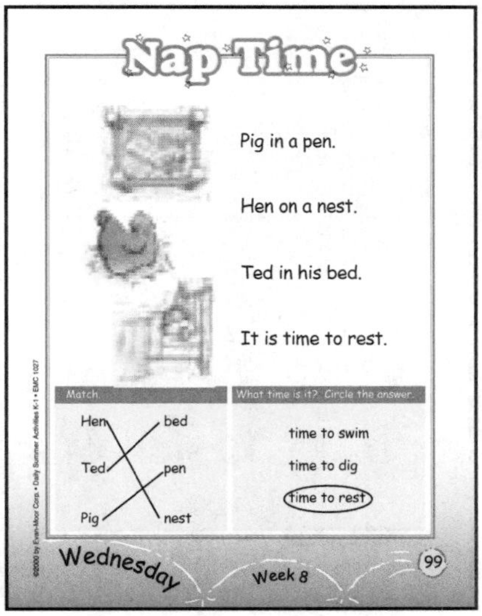

Page 100

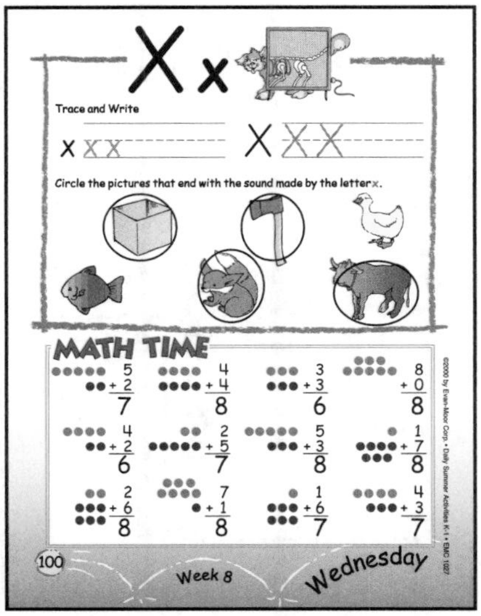

Page 101

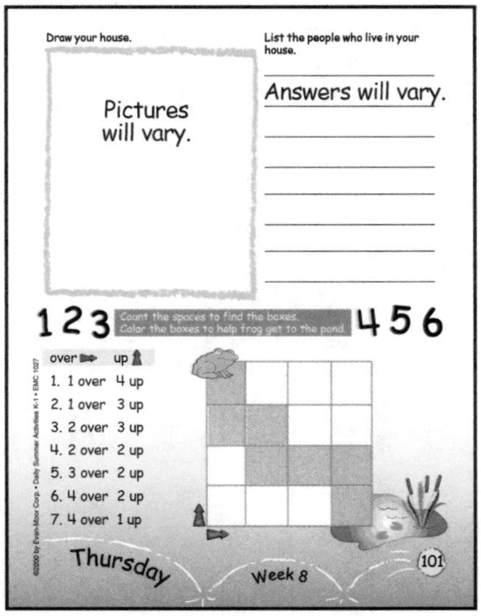

Page 102

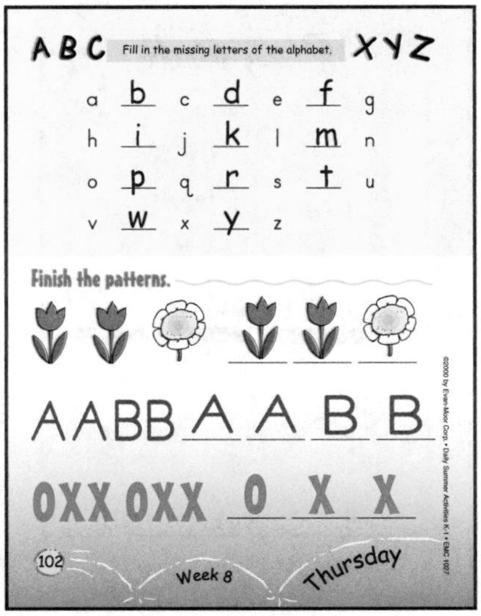

Page 103

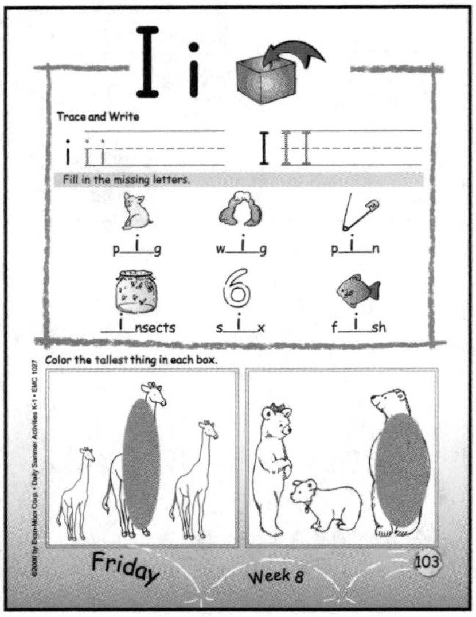

Page 104

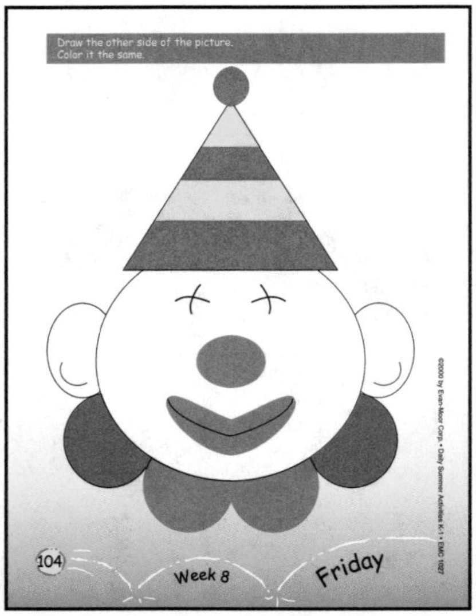

Page 107

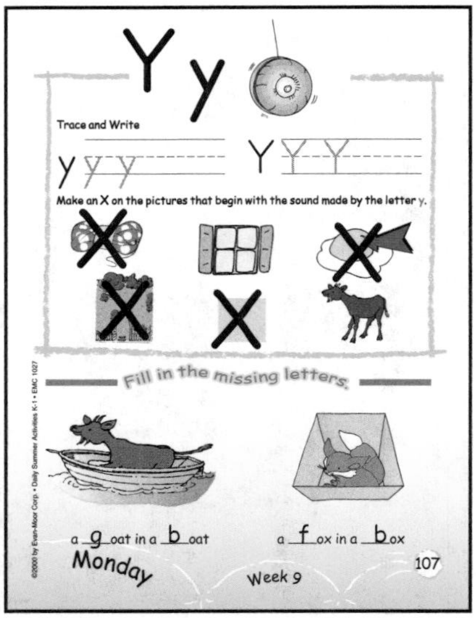

Page 108

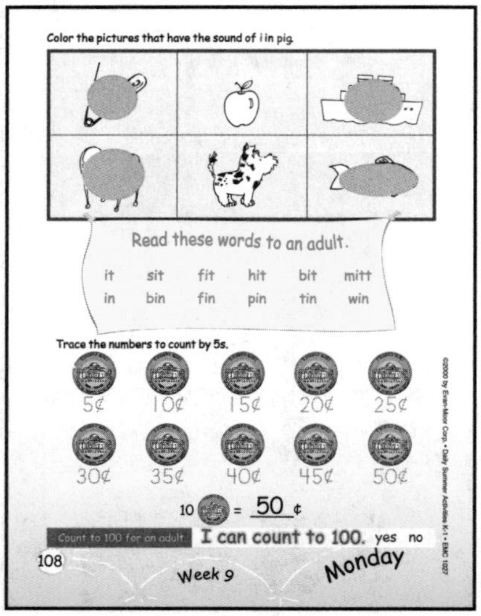

Page 109

Page 110

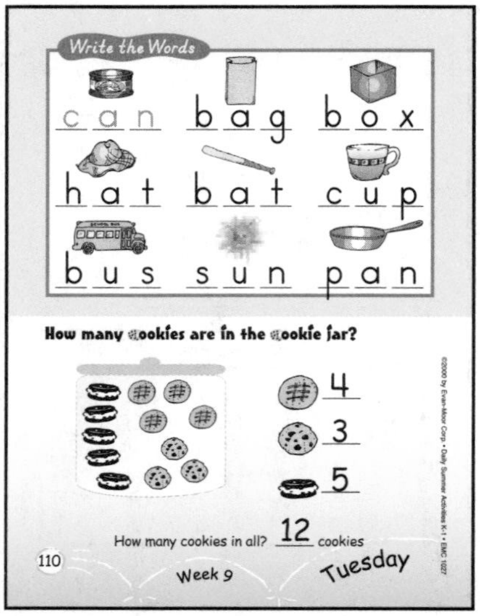

Page 111

Page 112

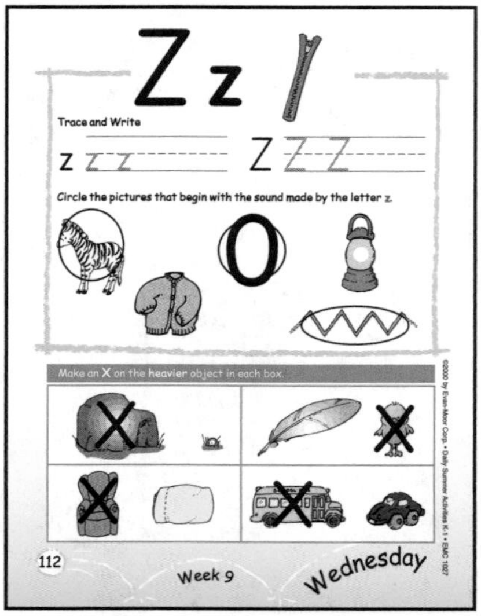

Page 113

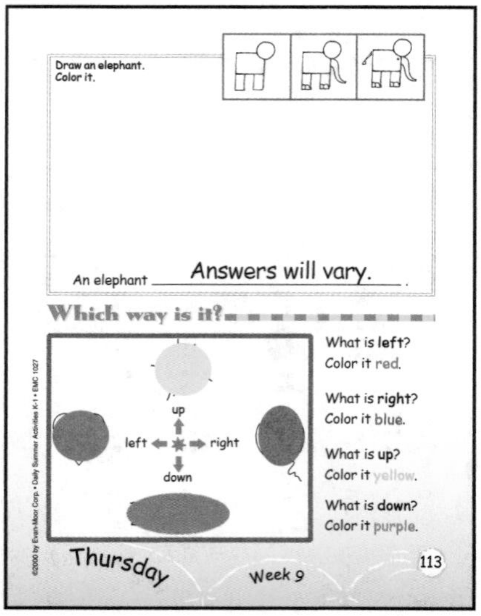

Page 114

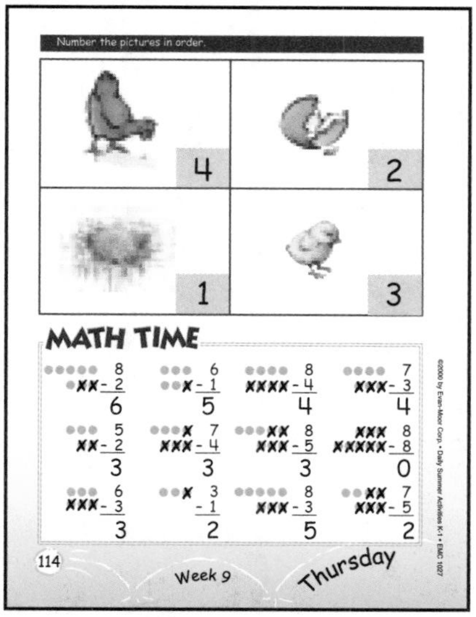
Number the pictures in order.

4 2
1 3

MATH TIME

8 - 2 = 6	6 - 1 = 5	8 - 4 = 4	7 - 3 = 4
5 - 2 = 3	7 - 4 = 3	8 - 5 = 3	8 - 8 = 0
6 - 3 = 3	3 - 1 = 2	8 - 3 = 5	7 - 5 = 2

114 Week 9 Thursday

Page 115

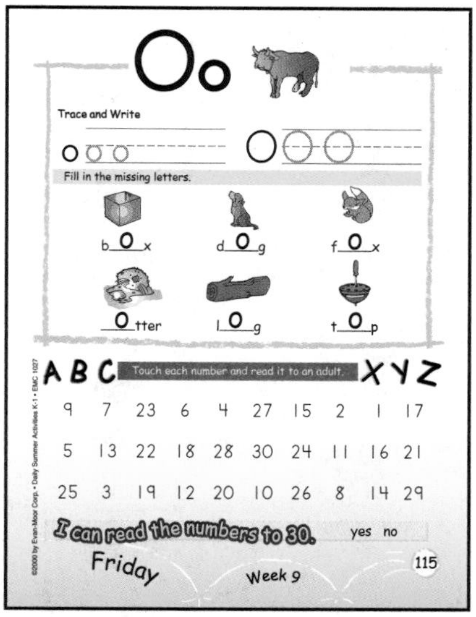
Oo

Trace and Write

o o o O O O

Fill in the missing letters.

box dog fox

otter log top

ABC Touch each number and read it to an adult. XYZ

9 7 23 6 4 27 15 2 1 17

5 13 22 18 28 30 24 11 16 21

25 3 19 12 20 10 26 8 14 29

I can read the numbers to 30. yes no

Friday Week 9 115

Page 116

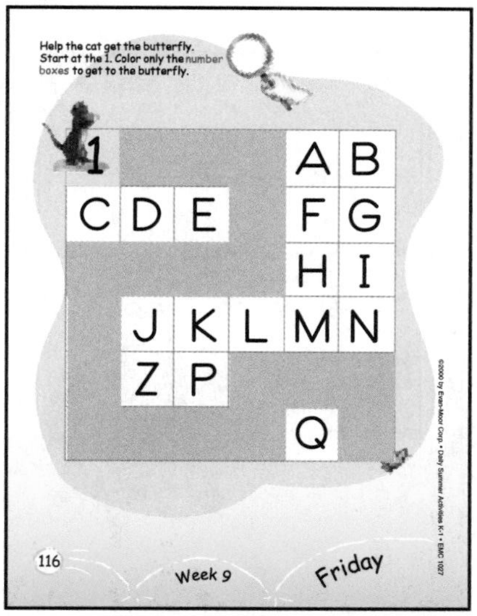
Help the cat get the butterfly. Start at the 1. Color only the number boxes to get to the butterfly.

1 A B C D E F G H I J K L M N Z P Q

116 Week 9 Friday

Page 119

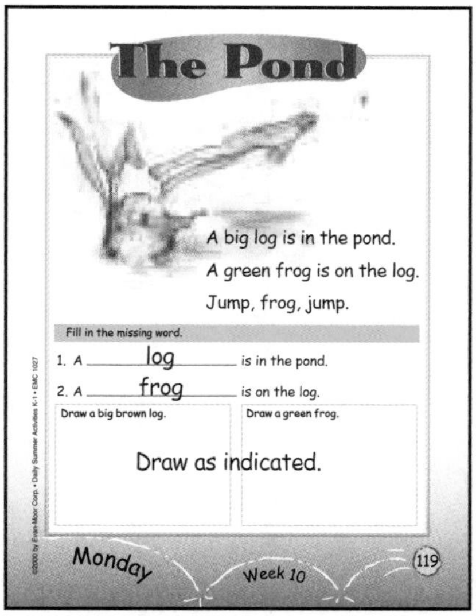
The Pond

A big log is in the pond.

A green frog is on the log.

Jump, frog, jump.

Fill in the missing word.

1. A log is in the pond.
2. A frog is on the log.

Draw a big brown log. Draw a green frog.

Draw as indicated.

Monday Week 10 119

Page 120

Uu

Trace and Write

u u u U U U

Fill in the missing letters.

sun bug bus

pup nuts cup

Make an X on the smaller insect in each box. Circle the bigger insect in each box.

120 Week 10 Monday

Page 121

Spell It! Practice spelling and and the.

Write a letter in each box.

and the

a n d t h e

Trace and write the words.

and and and

the the the

Copy the sentences using your best handwriting.

A toy fox is in that box.

A toy fox is in that box.

Six zebras are in the zoo.

Six zebras are in the zoo.

Tuesday Week 10 121

Page 122

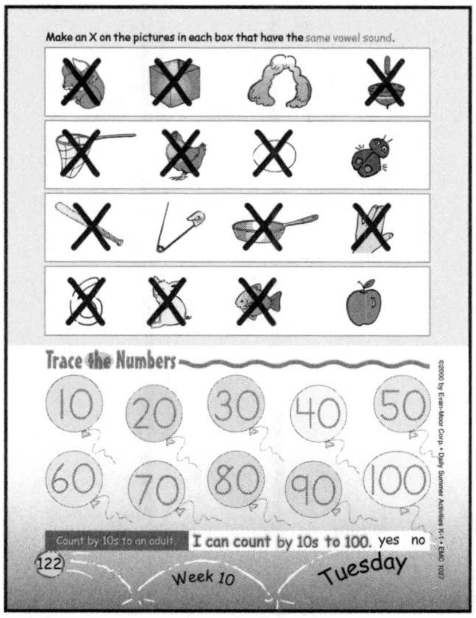
Make an X on the pictures in each box that have the same vowel sound.

Trace the Numbers

10 20 30 40 50 60 70 80 90 100

Count by 10s to an adult. I can count by 10s to 100. yes no

122 Week 10 Tuesday

Page 123

KIM

girl bath mud

Kim is a small girl.

She dug in the mud.

She is a mess.

Kim must take a bath.

Match the word to its picture.

Kim mud bath

Wednesday Week 10 123

Page 124

Color the pictures with the sound of u in cup.

How much money is in each purse?

20 ¢ 9 ¢

15 ¢ 30 ¢

124 Week 10 Wednesday

Page 125

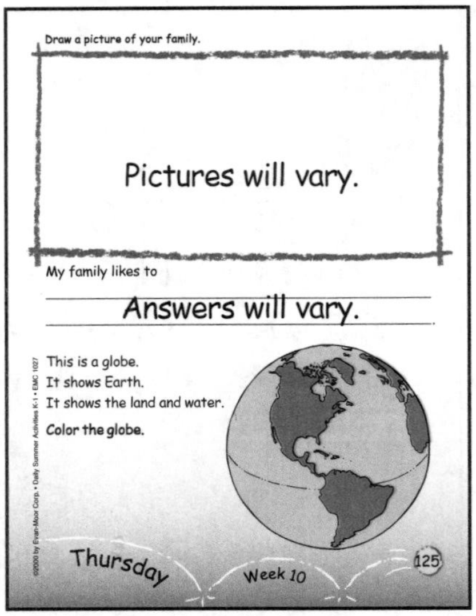
Draw a picture of your family.

Pictures will vary.

My family likes to

Answers will vary.

This is a globe.
It shows Earth.
It shows the land and water.

Color the globe.

Thursday Week 10 125

Page 126

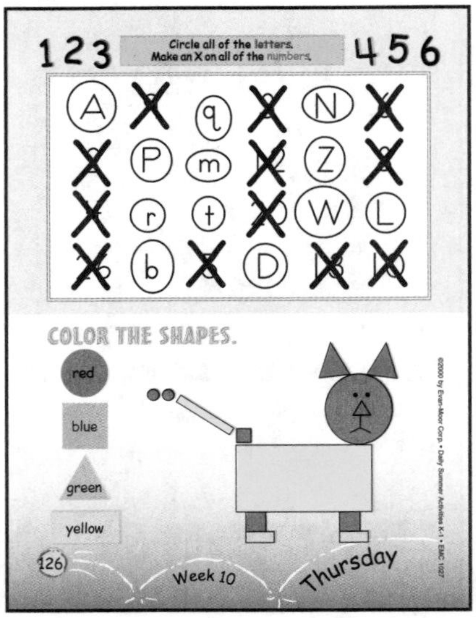
1 2 3 Circle all of the letters. Make an X on all of the numbers. 4 5 6

COLOR THE SHAPES.

red
blue
green
yellow

126 Week 10 Thursday

Page 127

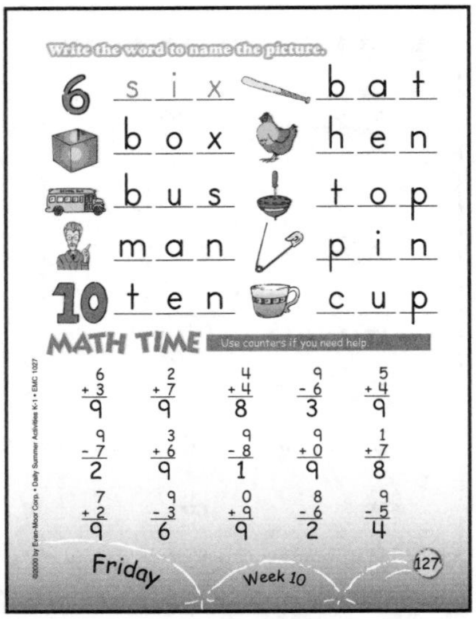
Write the word to name the picture.

six bat
box hen
bus top
man pin
ten cup

MATH TIME Use counters if you need help.

6 + 3 = 9	2 + 7 = 9	4 + 4 = 8	9 - 6 = 3	5 + 4 = 9
9 - 7 = 2	3 + 6 = 9	9 - 8 = 1	9 + 0 = 9	1 + 7 = 8
7 + 2 = 9	9 - 3 = 6	0 + 9 = 9	8 - 6 = 2	9 - 5 = 4

Friday Week 10 127

Page 128

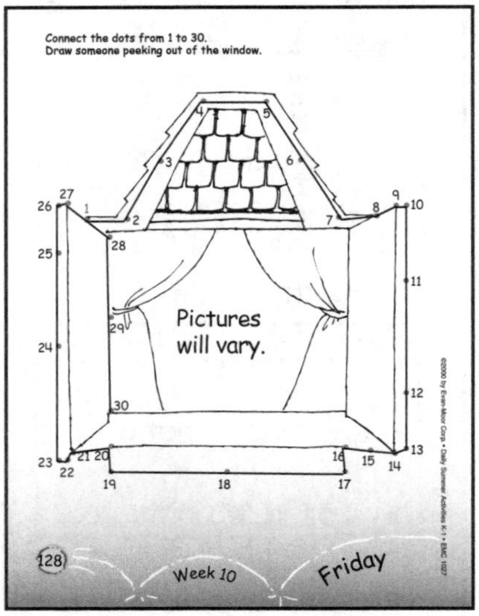
Connect the dots from 1 to 30.
Draw someone peeking out of the window.

Pictures will vary.

128 Week 10 Friday

Spell It!

This list contains all of the spelling words for weeks 1 through 10.

and	me
by	no
can	red
cat	run
dog	see
fast	six
go	stop
in	the
is	yes
jump	you